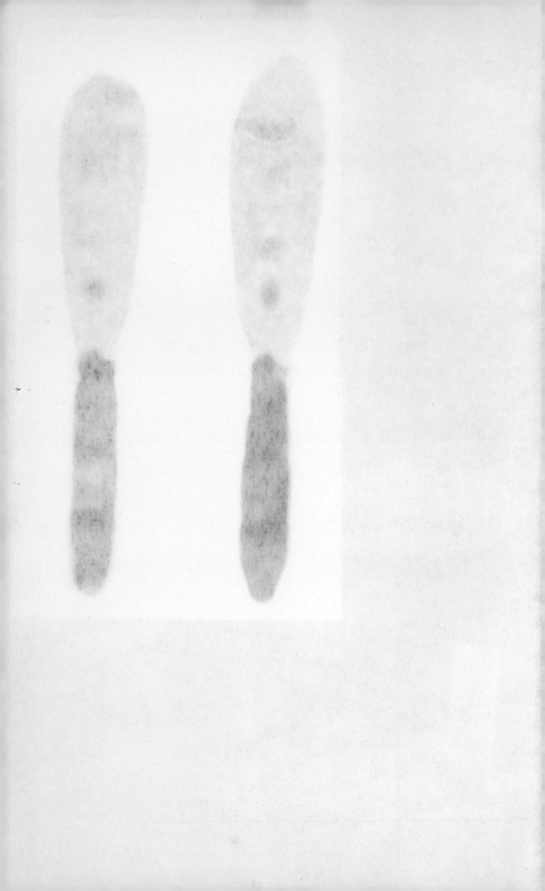

Earthly Delights,
Unearthly Adornments

# Books by Wright Morris

## *Novels*

THE FORK RIVER SPACE PROJECT
A LIFE
WAR GAMES
FIRE SERMON
IN ORBIT
ONE DAY
CAUSE FOR WONDER
WHAT A WAY TO GO
CEREMONY IN LONE TREE
LOVE AMONG THE CANNIBALS
THE FIELD OF VISION
THE HUGE SEASON
THE DEEP SLEEP
THE WORKS OF LOVE
MAN AND BOY
THE WORLD IN THE ATTIC
THE MAN WHO WAS THERE
MY UNCLE DUDLEY

## *Photo-Text*

LOVE AFFAIR: A VENETIAN JOURNAL
GOD'S COUNTRY AND MY PEOPLE
THE HOME PLACE
THE INHABITANTS

## *Essays*

EARTHLY DELIGHTS, UNEARTHLY ADORNMENTS
ABOUT FICTION
A BILL OF RITES, A BILL OF WRONGS, A BILL OF GOODS
THE TERRITORY AHEAD

## *Anthology*

WRIGHT MORRIS: A READER

## *Short Stories*

REAL LOSSES, IMAGINARY GAINS

Wright Morris

# Earthly Delights, Unearthly Adornments

## American Writers as Image-Makers

HARPER & ROW, PUBLISHERS
New York, Hagerstown, San Francisco, London

FIRST EDITION

*Designed by Stephanie Krasnow*

Library of Congress Cataloging in Publication Data
Morris, Wright, 1910—
   Earthly delights, unearthly adornments.
   Includes index.
   1. American literature—History and criticism.
2. Symbolism in literature. 3. Figures of speech.
4. English language style. I. Title.
PS169.S9M6   1978      810'.9      78-2154
ISBN 0-06-013107-1

 78 79 80 81 82 10 9 8 7 6 5 4 3 2 1

With grateful thanks to the National Endowment of the Humanities.

A longer version of "Origins" appeared in *Conversations with Wright Morris* published by the University of Nebraska Press, 1977.

AGAIN AND AGAIN
*for Jo*

# Contents

Earthly Delights,
Unearthly Adornments

# Of Memory, Emotion and Imagination

The small creatures of this world, and not a few of the large ones, are only at their ease under something. The cat crawls under the culvert, the infant under the table, screened off by the cloth that hangs like a curtain. In the Moldavanka ghetto of Odessa we have this self-portrait of Isaac Babel:

> As a boy I was given to lying. It was all due to reading. My imagination was always on fire. I read in class, during recess, on the way home, at night—under the dinner table, hidden by the folds of cloth that reached down to the floor. Reading made me miss all the important doings of this world.

In these few words much light is shed on the subject of fiction and the imagination. Not all writers burn with this fire, but many have their beginnings under something. Far from Odessa, in the Platte Valley of Nebraska, street culverts, piano boxes, the seats of wagons and buggies, railroad trestles, low bridges, the dark caves under front porches were all favored places of concealment. With Br'er Fox I shared the instinct to lie low. Seated in dust as fine as talcum, my lap and hands overlaid with a pattern of shadows, I peered out at the world through the holes between the slats. A train passed, a tethered cow mooed, a woman collected clothespins in the hammock of her apron, thunder crackled, rain puffed dust in the road, the bell tinkled on the Jewel's Tea Wagon as it crossed the tracks.

One reason I see it all so clearly is that I have so often put it into writing. Perhaps it is the writing I remember, the vibrant image I have made of the memory impression. A memory for just such details is thought to be characteristic of the writer, but the fiction is already at work in what he remembers. No deception is intended, but he wants to see clearly what is invariably, intrinsically vague. So he imagines. Image-making is indivisibly a part of remembering.

Not long ago I returned to the town I was born in, to the house I associated with my childhood. There were several, but *this* house was the house with the porch. From the conceal-ment of this porch I saw the train pass, I heard the cow moo and the thunder crackle, I watched the rain puff the dust in the road. To my puzzlement it proved to be a stoop less than a foot off the ground. A cat or a small dog might have crawled beneath it, but not a child. Brooding on this mystery, I began to recall under-the-porch furnishings I had conveniently for-gotten. There had been a pair of stilts, a scooter made from a fruit crate and a skate, a sled known as a Flexible Flyer Junior Racer, the wheels of a dismantled tricycle. Not this porch. *That* porch, indeed, had been five steps up from the walk to the porch, where a chain swing creaked and banged the clapboards. There *had* been a crosshatching of slats at one end, but the view had been blocked by the second-floor windows of a neighboring house. How was that possible? That porch was on a steep hill in the bluffs of Omaha, and not in the flatness of the Platte Valley. It had been a superior porch for conceal-ment and spying, and my imagination had shifted the scenery to suit the needs of fiction and emotion. I had substituted this more accommodating porch (with no loss in the quality of the dust, and a gain in furnishings and the height of the ceiling) for the one that my hometown had been lacking. I badly *wanted* that porch, and my imagination had obliged.

If I attempt to distinguish between fiction and memory, and press my nose to memory's glass to see more clearly, the remembered image grows more illusive, like the details in a Pointillist painting. I recognize it, more than I see it. The recognition is a fabric of emotion, as immaterial as music. In this defect of memory do we have the emergence of imagination? If we remembered both vibrantly and accurately—a documentary image rather than an impression—the imaginative faculty would be blocked, lacking the stimulus necessary to fill in what is empty or create what is missing. This faculty of artful lying is image-making, and not always confined to fiction writers. Precisely where memory is frail and emotion is strong, imagination takes fire.

One memory that is clear is that of a reader who took special pains to praise my memory, as evident in my fiction. He cited specific details from a number of novels: the white hairs from a mare's tail, a bent skate key, the cracked chimney of a lamp, a salvaged ball of tinfoil, and so on. I had heard this before. What led me to question it on that occasion? One novel in question, *Ceremony in Lone Tree,* was an assembly of parts from my own fictive archive. In the opening chapter, entitled "The Scene," many of these stray, unclaimed pieces found their ultimate and appropriate place. Somewhere in the past, memory had done its work, recording details from a variety of sources. From that album of objects and places I had selected the pieces appropriate to the fiction. Artifacts were jumbled with sensations. The cracked lamp of the chimney, in one place, gave rise to the smell of singed hair in another. That in turn to the fragrance of freshly dampened clothes, and the scorched smell of the iron. Fiction writers are often obsessed with a sense of place, and perhaps I am somewhat more obsessed than others. Most places have for me, in James's phrase, a sense of their own, a mystic meaning to give out.

To the extent one thing is almost like another, we are able to grasp, to reaffirm, both things. The overlapping of accumulated impressions gives depth and mystery to our experience with time. We have Proust's theme and variations on the inexhaustible Madeleine. The impressions of childhood, indelibly imprinted on a mind open and eager for sensations before it is cunningly attuned to ego satisfactions and evasions, are the ideal circumstances for the nature destined to be an image-maker. Adult impressions accumulate like the yearly fall of leaves, providing both protection and compost, waiting for the moment that the seedbed will sprout with its new growth. It will prove to be more than the writer had in mind, and much of it will be new.

For the American writer, more than most, repossession may be an act of re-creation. What was once there may have been little enough—or what was once there may have been obliterated. The furnishing of the mind with artifacts and symbols that began with Walt Whitman is increasingly a matter of salvage. The shortage of appropriately *saturated* artifacts is part of the deprivation felt by the younger generation. We all may miss, but hardly grow to cherish, what is felt to be intentionally obsolescent, instant *kitsch*.

In the craft of image-making there is much to be said for the slow grower. The less culture-shaped child, accumulating experience before he does art, when stimulated by the images of art will have recourse to his own unique resources. From Twain through Faulkner this has been a characteristic American experience. Those favored by a more cultivated background (like Henry James, or Edith Wharton) are felt to be less American. This is a narrow but telling distinction. The mind of James was shaped by the images of culture, rather than the rawer materials of experience. It is the purpose of culture to produce such minds, but a democratic culture has not evolved an appropriate use or place for them. Within the scope of a century, since Whitman, native raw materials have lost their rawness, and most writers of fiction have their beginnings as readers of fiction. It is the written image that now shapes the writer in his effort to become his own image-maker.

The observant child who grows up with paintings, the reflective child who grows up with books, is already at an artful remove from the natural surround of objects and places.

Later he may well experience a confusion of impressions. What was *real?* What had been imagined by somebody else? This is a tiresome but durable dilemma. Young Isaac Babel assures us that his imagination was enflamed by what he read, not by what he saw, but what he wrote tells us otherwise. He was pollinated from both sources. From the reading he received the emotional charge that fueled his feverish imagination. To a remarkable degree art produces art, and writing produces writers. Lack of originality in most image-makers has its roots in this imprinting. Only those with a very pronounced talent manage to depart from what they have received, and image what is their own. The cave painter also fell under this persuasion once he had a ceiling of images to inspire him, drawing what he beheld on the walls of the cave rather than the confusion and disorder of the hunt. We know that mimicry is crucial to learning, but those who learn it too early, or too well, may end up as duplicators, not image-makers. Image-making as distinct from likeness-making is illustrated in the description of a well-known public figure as one who has "a face like the bottom of a foot." This seemingly far-fetched comparison is an inspired piece of image-making: an original, not a duplication.

In his more buoyant moments the fiction writer knows that there is fiction quite beyond his conception, and his practice, but implicit in the nature of image-making. Of all this he has glimpses just beyond his grasping, teasingly beckoning and elusive. These glimpses go far to explain his romantic readiness for audacious gestures and strident manifestoes—as well as his irksome suspicion that he is in chains. The captivity of custom is so comprehensive the bonds that bind him also free and support him. He is aware of the world behind the Looking Glass but seems powerless to step through it. Space probers and great image-makers occupy the same void.

Almost a century ago Mark Twain greeted his readers:

NOTICE

Persons attempting to find a motive in this narrative will be prosecuted; persons attempting to find a moral in it will be banished; persons attempting to find a plot in it will be shot.

At˘the risk of being banished, few American writers have felt it safe to depart from the vernacular. All writers fell under the spell of the visible world, but only American writers had at their disposal a language seamlessly welded to their material— indeed, seemed to be the material itself, fraying away at the fringe of the immediate present.

> . . . Whatever may have been the case in years gone by, the true use for the imaginative faculty of modern times is to give ultimate vivification to facts, to science, and to common lives, endowing them with glows and glories and final illustriousness which belong to every real thing, and to real things only. Without that ultimate vivification—which the poet or other artist alone can give— reality would seem incomplete, and science, democracy, and life itself, finally in vain.

So Walt Whitman, in a loving all-embracing, backward glance.

# Closing the Gap

On a bench of planks, facing the sea, I share the view with a person unknown to me. Perhaps that is why I am at ease with him, and he is at ease with me. A gap of several feet exists between us as if reserved for a third party. Pigeons have sat there, otherwise it shows little wear. The sun shines, gulls dip and soar, the light over the sea glitters like sequins, but the space between us has not narrowed. The gap is an important part of the bench, a buffer zone.

Along the back of the bench the stranger's arm extends to within a foot or so of my shoulder. The weathered hand is freckled, with blunt fingers. Now and then it twitches, like a sunning lizard. If it should happen to touch me, we would both jump. His gaze appears to be fastened on the far blue horizon, but perhaps he naps. His nose is large, of the sort that bleeds when banged. More than like himself he looks old, as the young look young. In the folds of skin about his mouth stiff hairs grow out of the reach of his razor. One of his box-toed shoes has a knot in the laces. I check to see if his socks are mates. The large ear on my side is still growing and resembles a shell that is beached and hardening. It looks alive. I would hesitate to stoop and pick it up.

The gap between us is comforting, but suppose one of us felt the need to close it? How is that done? My father would have waved the newspaper he was holding, said aloud, "I see it's snowing back in Chicago." This gambit was known as breaking the ice. If broken, the stranger would contribute in a husky voice what was known about the weather in Knoxville, or Cedar Rapids. He had to be from somewhere else. Most Americans are. But once the weather had been discussed the break in the ice would seal over. The narrowing of the gap is permissible, but the closing of the gap was morally suspect. The bond one shared with a fellow creature was based on the gap's preservation. For my father, intimate knowledge of another person was a form of forbidden knowledge. He would have found self-revelation, as it is now practiced, indefensible. I am free of that superstition, but in its place I have acquired others. It has to do with images. If the image is right, is appropriate, what is revealed is acceptable. Image-making, quite frankly, is a form of magic. The image-maker is either involved with the enhancement of life, with its enlargement and dilation, or he contributes to its decline. In less ambitious terms, he either narrows or enlarges the gap.

This bench faces the sea, where a boat is passing, on which we are both, at this moment, departing. That, too, is a form of image-making. The whole world imagines what it must be like to arrive and depart. In a similar fashion I try to imagine the true nature of my companion. He is made of what little I see before me, and what shapes in my imagination. I have seen his likeness somewhere. Could it be in one of my own books? The way his crossed leg wags is familiar to me. He appears to me very like my *kind* of people, self-sufficient, self-deprived, self-unknowing—but of course these are fictions of my own contrivance. Seated here beside him, unknown to him, I am at ease in his silence. I know the type, if not the person. The gap between us is one that our natures mutually accept.

I have discovered that learning to *see* people is more difficult than learning to *know* them. The difficulty has a long history. Each of us must begin at the beginning. The appearance of grotesques may have its origins in the images recorded in childhood. What monsters we must be to the infant in the cradle, or the child that peers out from under the table where it feels safe. Little wonder that cartoons appeal to children if they approximate what they see. The hosts of adult caricatures in our frontier literature, a gallery of outsize giants and freaks, are grotesques of this order. What the child sees is less reassuring than what it feels, tastes and smells. The mother's "presence" is more substantial than the mother's image. The tactile senses are unquestioned, but what is seen begins and ends in illusion. Even for the older, experienced observer, recognition is a talent not to be taken for granted. To recognize a family likeness is a hard-won triumph. Creatures that know this better than we do rely on smell.

Bounced on the knee or held in the lap, the child fastens its gaze on the button that glitters, the chain that shines, the watch that ticks. In the father's vest pockets there are fountain pens with nickel clips, or indelible pencils with bright red caps. These pencils were forbidden, an added attraction. The bitter-tasting points were poisonous, if sucked on: the red color could be chewed or sucked off the caps. The button, the chain, the ticking watch, the pencils also held still for the child's examination. If its gaze lifted to the father's face, it saw an animated monster and noisemaker. Smoke often puffed from the nostrils or the mouth, like a dragon. Perhaps the maw spread wide, showing a cave with teeth. Little wonder the child shrieked with terror, or hid its face. The human face was an assembly of moving parts, staggering odors, deafening noises. It would not hold still to be seen and felt. It resisted the child's effort to taste it. Only the mother, with the child at her breast, could be experienced as a hovering, reassuring presence, the source of comforting sounds and agreeable flavors. Fathers were intricate. It would take time to see them, to taste them, to feel what they were like.

My father emerges, a piece at a time, from the scenic props of a blurred background, like those painted on the sets of a photographer's studio. There is a hand that dangles to where I can reach it, the fingers wriggling like live bait. I come to know that this signals, like a warning bell, that we are about to cross the railroad tracks. In semi-darkness, the movements jerky, as if he grappled with an invisible monster, I see him struggling, both hands at his throat, to attach or remove the high collar from which the ends of his tie dangle. Once detached, it will be stored for the night (the tie in it) on the curved post that supports the bureau mirror. The father's fingers smell of ink pads; there is a stain (from the indelible pencils) like a birthmark on his lips. He has a wheezing laugh, but he seems to be faceless until he is ill with erysipelas. A barber comes to the house to shave his head. My father sits on a chair, the pin-striped barber cloth concealing everything but his face. I am free to observe him. He does not look at me or speak. I soon turn away rather than admit to what it is I see.

This late refinement in my optical system paralleled my fresh awareness of the world around me. Through holes I rubbed in the winter-frosted windows I watched strangers pass, wearing masks like bandits. I learn the mask is worn to filter out the flu germs. Later I am awakened by the clanging of bells to see my father, in his nightshirt, hoisting the window. The clamor is deafening. Is it the end the world we have been expecting? No, it is merely the end of the war. Weighing myself on the scales in the depot lobby, I seem to lack interest in my own reflection. My phantom faceless presence hides in dark closets where I detect the smell of galoshes and a strange woman. I see my father's clenched-teeth smile. I see his head wag in a characteristic manner, as if buzzed by a fly. I see him in the darkness, candling eggs, the light flashing from the holes in the candler, but only now, sixty years later, do I wonder why he wears his rolled-brimmed fedora. The ladies admired his head of wavy brown hair.

The candling-room image is an assembly of overlapping, shifting memory impressions. It is one I have constructed to reaffirm and stabilize a fading impression. As a rule, this impression has displaced those more fleeting. But on occasion I detect something I had overlooked. My father chews on a sliver he has peeled from an egg case, and the front of his vest is strewn with packing excelsior. I see that clearly, but I am no longer sure if what I see is a fact or a fiction. With the purposeful exercise of memory, image-making has begun in earnest.

Here is an image that appears to be worn with handling. It is either colorless or the colors have faded. The elderly teacher with the grey face wears long strands of beads that gather in her lap when she is seated. They curl about her brown fingers when she is standing. In the spelldowns she stands near the cloakroom door where the hot air from the floor vent puffs out her skirts. After writing on the blackboard she blows the chalk dust from her fingers. She has her own chalk, because she doesn't like chalk that squeaks. When she has a headache, she must go and lie down on the cot in the nurse's room, off the annex, where her loose bone hairpins lie on the pillow. The closet in the annex smells of her rubbers and the apples in the pocket of her raincoat. The boy looking for the volleyball in the closet stands silent in the presence of more than he can see, less than he will remember. To make an image that is adequate to his sensations, he will have to imagine more than he remembers, intuit more than he saw.

Early memories, although lacking in detail, may be so charged with emotion they function as icons. Objects take precedence over people. Later memories are more "photogenic," as if we had learned to take better pictures.

Seated at a table in a cafeteria, I watch a small, frail woman, her hair in a tight bun, pushing through the swinging doors ahead of two boys. She wears a soiled raincoat over a house frock. The boys wear tennis sneakers without laces; otherwise they are stark naked. At a table the smaller boy sits crouched like a monkey, his legs drawn up. On his flat hairless chest long dark lashes have been added to the nipples, transforming them into eyes. His torso appears to be a white mask, the bellybutton a small fishlike mouth. Otherwise they are normal-looking bug-bitten boys, with straw-colored hair. The woman returns from the counter with coffee for herself, two jelly-topped rolls for the boys. They do not bolt their food: they eat it slowly, meditatively, like dessert. Both save the smear of jelly topping for the last bite. Neither the woman nor the boys feel they need to speak. They watch with interest as the busboy clears off the table, and lean away to make room as he swabs off the top. The woman's resemblance to the older boy is marked. Her face is free of makeup. The skin is taut as if put on the skull wet, then allowed to dry. They leave through a side door that does not revolve, and walk single file through rows of stalled traffic. I saw them clearly. I have described what I saw. But my imagination falters when confronted with such observable facts. We might say that life itself, in order to widen the gap the imagination is determined to close, is the most audacious and inexhaustible of all image-makers. Imagination is required if we are to admit to what we have seen.

But have we narrowed the gap? On the bench near the sea, although warmed by the sun, the two strangers are resigned to their separateness. Each, it would seem, has learned about people, the planet's most remarkable, thankless species. Pleasantries are all right, like music while eating, but intimacies too often lead to involvements. Only in the workshop of the imagination can these gaps be safely, and measurably, narrowed.

First time must pass, even appear to be lost, to generate the miracle of recovery. Time's unfinished business, the accumulated gaps of numberless, seemingly forgotten benches, patiently waits on the commingling of memory, emotion and imagination. Time salvaged from lost time is less time recovered than reconstituted. Of the making of time and images there will be no end.

# An Image Sampler

If the thought of the eye left Darwin cold all over, the thought of the "image" might have warmed and reassured him. Some sign, symbol or word is evoked by what is seen, thought, felt or heard. The relatively pure and immaterial world of music is a fabric of visual associations. Ballet constitutes its specific art form. Beethoven's *Pastoral*, Vivaldi's *Four Seasons*, Debussy's *Images* testify to our compelling need to see what is invisible. The poet, the painter, the physicist, the chemist and Madame Sosostris, famous clairvoyante, all strain to *see*. In range and variety images made with words may exceed those drawn, calculated or constructed.

> Weapon shapely, naked, wan,

is a deftly stroked *image* of an axe head. In economy, in incisiveness, this approximates an ideogram, a Chinese character. Whitman's image is remarkably vibrant, but it requires imagination to see it. To be seen, it must still be shaped on the mind's eye.

> The regiment bled extravagantly. Grunting bundles of blue began to drop.

This was not the customary image of war at the time it was written. The beast of war is seen as an aggregate creature, one

13

part of which bleeds extravagantly. Bundles of blue, like fur tufts, drop from its hide. The words and syntax are simple. The originality is in the image. Although Stephen Crane was inexperienced with war, his view was as Olympian as Zeus.

The complexity of the word image is that it may be external and internal at once, presenting both a "picture" and a state of being.

> Anna found her place with large, abundant women, for such were always lazy, careless or all helpless, and so the burden of their lives could fall on Anna, and give her just content.

The appeal that defies analysis is in the simplicity and music of the language, resulting in style. This style is exceptional in the way it awakens the half-aware, long-dormant reader. He reads again what he has just read, dimly aware that something has escaped him. That something is the presence of the author in the style. Gertrude Stein herself is aware, and she is eager to share this awareness with the reader.

> Why did absence of light disturb him less than presence of noise?
> Because of the surety of the sense of touch in his firm full masculine feminine passive active hand.

These lines from James Joyce are not easily *imaged*. The interested reader must keep his focus on the words themselves. The sensation is largely verbal, and resists the effort to make it visual. The difficulties readers find in darkest James and deepest Joyce often lie in the abstract nature of their images, the resistance they offer to verbalization.

> —Good marrams, sagd he, freshwatties and boasterdes all, as he put into bierhiven, nogeysokey first, cabootle segund, jilling to windwards, as he made straks for that oerasound the snarsty weg for Publin, so was his horenpipe lug in the lee off their mouths organs, with his tilt too taut for his tammy all a slaunter and his wigger on a wagger with its tag tucked.

Dissolved in the acid of Joyce's wit and wordplay, the image resists reassembly, not unlike the parts of a Cubist painting. In

Joycese we are involved with the primal ooze of language. It may well be an anti-image, having in mind a fresh start with the first play of light on the waters, with God saying, "Let there be light," and the light was Joyce. He never lacked for audacity, but it led him to overestimate his readers.

Henry James wrote:

> . . . She only kept him waiting, however; that is he only waited. It had become suddenly, from her movement and attitude, beautiful and vivid to him that she had something more to give him; her wasted face delicately shone with it—it glittered almost as with the white luster of silver in her expression. She was right, incontestably, for what he saw in her face was the truth, and strangely, without consequence, while their talk of it as dreadful was still in the air, she appeared to present it as inordinately soft. This, prompting bewilderment, made him but gape the more gratefully for her revelation. . . .

The reader, too, is prompted to bewilderment to seize on this description. The problem lies in how to image the *presentiment* that something will, or must, happen. In what we read the pump is primed, and primed, but nothing comes up. It is the writer's intent to frustrate the character, but he ends in also frustrating the reader. The image appropriate to this mutual frustration is not forthcoming.

Conrad writes:

> Mr. Verloc was going westward through a town without shadows in an atmosphere of powdered gold.

This single line is not as unmistakably Conrad as the previous quotation was unmistakably James, but both writers are traditional in style and make no bows to the vernacular. The line is shaped to please a cultivated taste, rather than arouse or provoke it. The tale itself might be daring and innovative, but it is not evident in the syntax. Whitman, Crane, Stein and Joyce depart from this tone in the interests of a greater verisimilitude. The spoken language is emerging as the language of the tribe. It opens the door on the brawling extremes to which neither the reader nor the writer will for long be accustomed, and it closes the door, firmly, on the materials of image-making sold over the counter. Like the painter, the writer is his own image-maker.

The poet writes:

Let us go then, you and I,
When the evening is spread out against the sky
Like a patient etherised upon a table . . .

The storyteller:

. . . The children's mother still had on slacks and still had her head tied up in a green kerchief, but the grandmother had on a navy blue straw sailor hat with a bunch of white violets on the brim and a navy blue dress with a small white dot in the print. Her collar and cuffs were white organdy trimmed with lace and at her neckline she had pinned a purple spray of cloth violets containing a sachet. In case of an accident, anyone seeing her dead on the highway would know at once that she was a lady.

Fifty years of distinguished vernacular writing contribute to the style of Flannery O'Connor. The tone is her own, a unique commingling of immediacy and detachment, the commonplace and the prodigious. The last line is a masterly summation of what is omnipresent but unstated. That this condition is revealed as comically bizarre is the marvel of O'Connor's talent. It is unthinkable, it is *unimaginable,* in a pre-vernacular language.

He started going into this nodding routine. You never saw anybody nod as much in your life as old Spencer did. You never knew if he was nodding a lot because he was thinking and all, or just because he was a nice old guy that didn't know his ass from his elbow.

This is the world of Holden Caulfield. As Twain was the first to demonstrate, the vernacular is peculiarly sympathetic to the nature of adolescent experience: in particular American adolescent experience.

We danced about four numbers. In between numbers she's funny as hell. She stays right in position. She won't even talk or anything. You both have to stay right in position and wait for the orchestra to start playing again. That kills me. You're not supposed to laugh or anything, either.

The gift of hope, the extravagant highs and lows, even the texture and pacing of the interior monologue lends itself to vernacular exaggeration. Every circumstance, as in frontier humor, teeters toward an excessive response. Ring Lardner's "I can't breathe!" is replaced by "That kills me." The bright and shiny portraits of adolescence are still among the chief ornaments of American fiction, a fact we owe in part to the nature of our culture, but chiefly to the remarkable language of the tribe. The romantic readiness persists as adolescence fades. Both Stephen Dedalus and Augie March prepare themselves for life with images.

Modern literature is largely identified with three non-American masters, Proust, Joyce and Mann, but the renaissance of image-making of the twentieth century is largely of vernacular inspiration. This triumph has had its consequences, and I have discussed some of them in *About Fiction*. In the ceaseless brawl of a common and abused language, increasingly the property of media promotion, a clearing must once more be made, as in a jungle, where the language can be used and nurtured. The overwhelming prevalence of the "likeness," the "representation," through the photograph, the movies, the surround of television, is modifying our besieged and drugged natures in ways too cunning and insidious to measure. These *images* for many have already displaced reality. Once the sole preserve of the imagination, and recognized with fear and trembling as holy, the image-making faculty is now part of the media massage. We can speak of this as corruption of the well at its source.

fiction, and gives a foretaste of its nature. Drizzly November still dominates this writer's soul, but he has come far from the ports of high adventure.

And yet it hardly seems the tone of a writer who has just passed his thirty-fifth birthday. The Ishmael in his nature has had its say, and he is at that point in the middle of life that approximates a balance. Melancholy has not yet hung him with the mourning weeds that festoon the letters of the *San Dominick*, the ship under the command of Benito Cereno. Melville is of a mood to go to sea, but his ship is now his study. He is at the summit of his craft, but he sees the world something more than darkly, being one who, however briefly, on honeydew had fed and drunk the milk of paradise. His religious doubts—confessed to Hawthorne—the perplexities he had observed in human nature and customs, were of the sort he could neither resign himself to nor reject. By temperament he appeared to be one of those chosen to suffer the torments of the age, rather than resolve them. The dilemma of race and color, of master and slave—one that will change its aspect but not its nature—has no more profound depiction than we find in "Benito Cereno." As in "Bartleby, the Scrivener," Melville fully anticipates what we assume to be a modern predicament.

But my concern is with the image-maker. He describes the slave ship in this manner:

> The tops were large, and were railed about with what had once been octagonal net-work, all now in sad disrepair. These tops hung overhead like three ruinous aviaries, in one of which was seen perched, on a ratlin, a white noddy, a strange fowl, so called from its lethargic somnambulistic character, being frequently caught by hand at sea. Battered and mouldy, the castellated forecastle seemed some ancient turret, long ago taken by assault, and then left to decay. Towards the stern, two high-raised quarter galleries—the balustrades here and there covered with dry, tindery sea-moss—opening out from the unoccupied state-cabin, whose dead lights, for all the mild weather, were hermetically sealed and caulked—these tenantless balconies hung over the sea as if it were the grand Venetian canal. But the principal relic of

faded grandeur was the ample oval of the shield-like stern-piece, intricately carved with the arms of Castile and Leon, medallioned about by groups of mythological or symbolical devices; uppermost and central of which was a dark satyr in a mask, holding his foot on the prostrate neck of a writhing figure, likewise masked.

Much of that is contrived to suit the tale, but it preserves the quality of close observation. Only from a man saturated with sea lore would these details come so readily. In passages of this nature we can sense the writer's pleasure in image-making that gratifies on many levels. In these imaginings he reinhabits the world of his heart's longing, with the perplexities scaled to a slave ship becalmed in a bay off the coast of Chile.

> Always upon first boarding a large and populous ship at sea, especially a foreign one, with a nondescript crew such as Lascars or Manilla men, the impression varies in a peculiar way from that produced by first entering a strange house with strange inmates in a strange land. Both house and ship, the one by its walls and blinds, the other by its high bulwarks like ramparts, hoard from view their interiors till the last moment; but in the case of the ship there is this addition: that the living spectacle which it contains, upon its sudden and complete disclosure, has, in contrast with the blank ocean which zones it, something of the effect of enchantment. The ship seems unreal; these strange costumes, gestures, and faces, but a shadowy tableau just emerged from the deep, which directly must receive back what it gave.

This prepared ground, for one agreeable to it, is the equal to many months at sea, and shapes the mind to absorb and ponder the unreal events that soon follow. Intuitive rightness of scene spares the writer and reader the strain of demonstration. Few readers would guess what a Lascar is, or a sailor freak, or a ratlin, or a white noddy, but in the context of Melville's description we are intrigued and lured on by what eludes us, even grateful for our amateur status. The writer speaks of what he knows. The white noddy, perched on the ratlin, gleams the brighter, thanks to our ignorance.

We know how deeply Melville read Shakespeare, and how

that music on occasion overwhelmed his own, but the objects and places of his imagination derive from his years at sea. The bookish and metaphysical sides of his nature sometimes clog his narration but they do not obscure his vision. This is of images compact, crystallizing the impressions of all men who stroll up and down beaches, pace the decks of cruise ships or find themselves, when it is drizzly in their souls, contemplating a sea voyage.

> . . . Let the most absent-minded of men be plunged in his deepest reveries—stand that man on his legs, set his feet a-going, and he will infallibly lead you to water, if water there be in all that region. . . .Yes, as everyone knows, meditation and water are wedded forever.

Fortunately, Melville's unique gift for image-making spared the world many tomes of heavy-laden metaphysics, the weather in his soul increasingly black as he endured the life of a landsman.

> It is strange how he persists [Hawthorne wrote] and has persisted ever since I knew him, and probably long before—in wandering to and fro over these deserts, as dismal and monotonous as sandhills amid which we were sitting. He can neither believe, nor be comfortable in his unbelief; and he is too honest and courageous not to try to do one or the other.

Unschooled in metaphysical thought, Melville pondered metaphysics in his images:

> Who in the rainbow can draw the line where the violet tint ends and the orange tint begins? Distinctly we see the difference of the colour, but where exactly does the one visibly enter into the other?

These are lines from *Billy Budd,* his last book. The logical mind, the logical faculty of the mind, is exercised to make distinctions that may or may not exist in nature. Man's moral nature, to the extent that he is human, is a spectrum of hues so commingled that fine distinctions are purely arbitrary. What is good and what is evil, what is true and what is false, is neither violet nor orange but the prismatic aurora we glimpse fitfully, at sunrise, caught in the fleece of low-lying clouds. An observant eye might capture, in an image, how this fact of nature parallels human nature, testifying to that faculty of mind we describe as imagination.

# Whitman

Come for a stroll with me, the voice whispers, and I feel his hand cradling my elbow. He walks less than he saunters, he saunters less than he stands or sits observing. With a genial side glance he checks to see if I see what he is seeing. The glance of an accomplice, before the greatest show on earth.

Mild, foolish, dough-colored, simpering face; black cloth suit—shad-bellied, single-breasted coat, with low standing collar all round, vest buttoned close to throat, knees a little bent, toes turned out, and chin down. Episcopalian deacon.

Wild cataract of hair; absurd, bunged-up felt hat, with peaked crown; velvet coat, all friggled over with gimp, but worn; eyes rather staring, look upward. Third-rate artist.

Half-a-dozen ill-dressed fellows together (this in the evening); dirty, unshorn faces; debauched expression; the half-shut eyes, and loose, hanging lips of the tribe; hoarse voices, incredibly tuneless; oaths and curses; laughs made up of a yell and a cackle; a peculiar quick, eager step, as they flock along close together. Short-boys; damnable dangerous villains.

Dirty finery, excessively plentiful; paint, both red and white; draggle-tailed dress, ill-fitting; coarse features, unintelligent; bold glance, questioning, shameless, perceptibly anxious; hideous croak or dry, brazen ring in voice; affected, but awkward, mincing, waggling gait. Harlot.

These are the "uniforms" of the tribes. He also has an eye for the individual.

> A tall, slender man, round-shouldered, chin stuck out, deep-set eyes, sack-coat. His step is quick, and his arms swing awkwardly, as if he were trying to knock his elbows together behind him. Albert Brisbane, the Socialist . . .

> Somebody in an open barouche, driving daintily. He looks like a doll; is it alive? We'll cross the street and so get close to him. Did you see? Fantastic hat, turned clear over in the rim above the ears; blue coat and shiny brass buttons; patent leathers; shirt-frill; gold specs; bright red cheeks, and singularly definite jetty black eyebrows, moustache, and imperial. You could see that from the sidewalk; but you saw, when you stood at his wheel, not only the twinkling diamond ring and breast-pin, but the heavy slabby red paint; and even the substratum of the grizzly grey under that jetty dye. . . . The Baron Spolasco, with no end of medical diplomas . . .

There are of course many others, but here is an odd one:

> Tall, large, rough-looking man, in a journeyman carpenter's uniform. Coarse, sanguine complexion; strong, bristly, grizzled beard; singular eyes, of a semi-transparent, indistinct light blue, and with that sleepy look that comes when the lid rests half way down over the pupil; careless, lounging gait. Walt Whitman, the sturdy self-conscious microcosmic, prose-poetical author of that incongruous hash of mud and gold—*Leaves of Grass.*

Do we get the picture? It is drawn, like the others, from long and careful observation. Nor would he, like another, sing so much of himself if there was anybody else he knew as well. Walt Whitman, that cosmos, is a breed of man that might have interested Audubon, the painter of native birds. Here was one with a notable span of wing, unusual feathering and a distinctly characteristic song. He will himself refer to it as a "barbaric yawp." Birds of this type were to be found in the woods, and the woodwork, that now spanned the continent westward. They would soon be described by a new breed of writers, using this new breed of language.

In the sketches I have quoted, Whitman's talents appear to

be novelistic. His eye is sharp. The language is tailored to the subject. They appear to be quick portraits taken from life that will soon make their way into fiction. He not merely images what he sees, but he has the gift of characterization. Surely there is a story in that tribe of young villains with their tuneless voices, their debauched expressions. The casual, deceptively offhand manner is image-making, as well as duplicating. The writer's long experience with magazines and newspapers can be seen in the concise, economical style. He is at ease with prose, but the brevity of these sketches is instructive. He wants the exact image more than he does the "story."

> I saw the marriage of the trapper in the open air in the far west, the bride was a red girl, her father and his friends sat near cross-legged and dumbly smoking, they had moccasins to their feet and large thick blankets hanging from their shoulders, on a bank lounged the trapper, he was drest mostly in skins, his luxuriant beard and curls protected his neck, he held his bride by the hand, she had long eyelashes, her head was bare, her coarse straight locks descended upon her voluptuous limbs and reach'd to her feet.

The writer's eye for detail is the same, but his style has altered. The short staccato phrases, the adjectives and semicolons, have given way to a long rolling line that has no metered cadence. It takes repeated readings to get the hang of it, to see the look of it. Perhaps it helps if we see it like this:

I saw the marriage of the trapper in the open air in the far west, the bride was a red girl,
Her father and his friends sat near cross-legged and dumbly smoking, they had moccasins to their feet and large thick blankets hanging from their shoulders,
On a bank lounged the trapper, he was drest mostly in skins, his luxuriant beard and curls protected his neck, he held his bride by the hand,
She had long eyelashes, her head was bare, her coarse straight locks descended upon her voluptuous limbs and reach'd to her feet.

These lines are devoid of both common and uncommon

notions of rime and meter. The rhythm might come from the voice of the speaker. The narrative manner is oracular, straightforward, with the parts taking their place in proportion to the whole. The exceptional freedom of this "form" is exhilarating, but it encouraged the excesses and banalities that clutter up much of Whitman's work. It also provided the appropriate canvas for his gifts as an image-maker.

The big doors of the country barn stand open and ready,
The dried grass of the harvest-time loads the slow-drawn wagon,
The clear light plays on the brown gray and green intertinged,
The armfuls are pack'd to the sagging mow.

The first to inventory the visible New World, Whitman was overwhelmed by its abundance. The long affectionate listings are those of a Noah who records the contents of his ark. Forget the refinements: identify with it!

The blab of the pave, tires of carts, sluff of boot-soles, talk of the promenaders,
The heavy omnibus, the driver with his interrogating thumb, the clank of the shod horses on the granite floor,
The snow-sleighs, clinking, shouted jokes, pelts of snow-balls,
The hurrahs for popular favorites, the fury of rous'd mobs,
The flap of the curtain'd litter, a sick man inside borne to the hospital . . .

This quick seizure and appraisal is that of an observer who is all eyes and fumbling hands. Occasionally he perceives a new species.

Weapon shapely, naked, wan,
Head from the mother's bowels drawn,
Wooded flesh and metal bone, limb only one and lip only one . . .

This *likeness* would surely puzzle the woodsman and such a user of axes as Thoreau. Here is a blade that cuts more than ordinary. The new language, in this example, has proved adequate to the new vista.

The spotted hawk swoops by and accuses me, he complains of my gab and my loitering.

I too am not a bit tamed, I too am untranslatable,
I sound my barbaric yawp over the roofs of the world.

The last scud of day holds back for me,
It flings my likeness after the rest and true as any on the shadow'd
    wilds,
It coaxes me to the vapor and the dusk.

Walt Whitman, born in May, 1819, died in March, 1892.

Herman Melville, born in August, 1819, died in September,
1891.

To our knowledge they were ignorant of each other. How
inscrutably American that is! How, image-makers, make an
image of that? Mark Twain was aware of Whitman, the poet,
but we do not know that he read *Leaves of Grass*, considered
both strong and tainted medicine. These self-schooled voices
remained unrelated in the rising din of the gilded age,
wilderness howls and strident urban clamor. Their separateness had much to do with what was unique and original in
their respective talents. Each writer made the most of his own
limited resources. The sea provided Melville, as it did Conrad,
with a mirror adequate to his moral insights, the way the
thronging streets and byways nourished Whitman's "Democratic Vistas." Novelty is on the side of Whitman, focus and
intensity on the side of Melville. The sea has always been
there, inspiring and intimidating, but it has few creatures as
strange as this one:

The smoke of my own breath,
Echoes, ripples, buzz'd whispers, love-root, silk thread crotch and
    vine,
My respiration and inspiration, the beating of my heart, the passing
    of blood and air through my lungs,
The sniff of green leaves and dry leaves, and of the shore and dark-
    color'd sea rocks, and of hay in the barn,
The sound of the belch'd words of my voice loos'd to the eddies of
    the wind . . .

It is curious how the lover of the common man, "the bulk-
people of all lands, the women not forgetting," is so often the

embryonic superman. Fortunately, the deep compassionate gentleness of Whitman's nature made him more the earth mother than the machismo male. He embraced rather than ruled. Nor did his love for his self-image eventually gall and disgust him; on his old bones the flesh retained its sweetness. Was it self-love that sustained his faith in the common man that Twain would soon describe as "human muck"? As a postscript to his last letter he wrote:

> . . . More & more it comes to the fore that the only theory worthy our modern times for g't literature politics and sociology must combine all the bulk-people of all lands, the women not forgetting. But the mustard plaster on my side is stinging & I must stop—Goodby to all.

Of the great figures of his time Whitman alone retained his optimism. He alone, at the middle of his life, fashioned a credo from which he never departed. In the preface to *Leaves of Grass* he wrote:

> . . . This is what you shall do: Love the earth and sun and the animals, despise riches, give alms to every one that asks, stand up for the stupid and crazy, devote your income and labor to others, hate tyrants, argue not concerning God, have patience and indulgence toward the people, take off your hat to nothing known or unknown, or to any man or number of men—go freely with powerful uneducated persons, and with the young, and with the mothers of families—re-examine all you have been told in school or church or in any book, and dismiss whatever insults your own soul; and your very flesh shall be a great poem, and have the richest fluency, not only in its words, but in the silent lines of its lips and face, and between the lashes of your eyes, and in every motion and joint of your body. . . .

This is a rhetoric of nouns and declarative statements. If it is put down in the manner of his poetry:

This is what you shall do:
Love the earth and sun and the animals, despise riches, give alms to
  every one that asks,
Stand up for the stupid and crazy, devote your income and labor to
  others,

Hate tyrants, argue not concerning God, have patience and indul-
  gence toward the people,
Take off your hat to nothing known or unknown, or
To any man or number of men.
Go freely with powerful uneducated persons, and with the young,
  and with the mothers of families,

And so on. It proves to be better than some of the poems, but
less good than the best. The urgency, the directness of statement, the eagerness of shared truth, a shared experience, the
tone of the affectionate seer and guru who walks with us as he
talks, his hand on our shoulder or about our waist.

Behold, I do not give lectures or a little charity,
When I give I give of myself.

Whitman's audacity as an innovator is matched by his
candor. Only the fact that he went unread spared him the
abuses of an outraged public. Surely this old man—and he
aged early; the image of the bearded seer was agreeable to
him—could not be guilty of the rumored charges.

I have perceiv'd that to be with those I like is enough,
To stop in company with the rest at evening is enough,
To be surrounded by beautiful, curious, breathing, laughing flesh is
  enough,
To pass among them or touch any one, or rest my arm ever so lightly
  round his or her neck for a moment, what is this then?
I do not ask any more delight, I swim in it as in a sea.

This poem drooping shy and unseen that I always carry, and that all
  men carry . . .
Love-thoughts, love-juice, love-odor, love-yielding, love-climbers,
  and the climbing sap,
Arms and hands of love, lips of love, phallic thumb of love, breasts of
  love, bellies press'd and glued together with love,
Earth of chaste love, life that is only after love.

It is hard to appreciate, more than a century later, the
scandalous power of such words at the time they were published. Melville would have found confirmation of what he
hinted at, darkly, and Twain would have been horrified.

Whitman's fervor cooled as he grew older, and to a friend in London he confessed to being the father of two illegitmate children, deceased, in this way squaring his image as a man among men. From Whitman these fictions are one of the affected touches to a familiar and much loved portrait. Years before, he had darkly suggested a love affair with an octoroon in New Orleans—conveniently at a remove from New York and New Jersey—as later young men would boast of amorous intrigues in Paris. It is the last of his poses, an old man's touching admission that his public and final image perhaps lacked something. Those who know and love him will doubt that, taking him at his word that he is a man of many contradictions.

Perhaps the well-projected self-image is crucial to American optimism. Mark Twain was of this breed when he began his apprenticeship as a river pilot, a brief period of recovery and repossession that would reach its climax in *Huck Finn,* a late song to himself. But before he had finished the book, shadows clouded the boy's adventure. The author's great expectations float down the river with Jim, into slavery. Both Twain and Whitman were songbirds, shamelessly self-celebrating, the natural drift of their talents infectiously life-enhancing, but they grew separate and unequal in what they expected, and what they acknowledged.

# Mark Twain

... I can call back the solemn twilight and mystery of the deep woods, the earthy smells, the faint odors of the wild flowers, the sheen of rain-washed foliage, the rattling clatter of drops when the wind shook the trees, the far-off hammering of woodpeckers and the muffled drumming of wood pheasants in the remoteness of the forest, the snapshot glimpses of disturbed wild creatures scurrying through the grass—I can call it all back and make it as real as it ever was, and as blessed. I can call back the prairie, and its loneliness and peace, and a vast hawk hanging motionless in the sky, with his wings spread wide and the blue of the vault showing through the fringe of their end feathers. I can see the woods in their autumn dress, the oaks purple, the hickories washed with gold, the maples and sumachs luminous with crimson fires, and I can hear the rustle made by the fallen leaves as we plowed through them ...

In its fervor, this inventory of a bountiful nature recalls Whitman. The pronoun "I" predominates, and the author is at pains to exercise his total recall. As the memories come flooding back, one linked to the other, he gives himself over to the flow of impressions. It is consistently euphoric, an idyll of pastoral bliss, the "very heaven" of a boy's imagination, with no palpable hint of the terrors that are known to lurk in the frontier woodwork, real and imaginary. The reader has been lifted to the author's lap, where he is empowered to become enchanted. Neither the author nor the listener questions the spell that is intended. Back there in time, as well as in space, was the Great Good Place. Give or take a few birds, a few trees, a few berries, that's how it was. Far enough *back* there to be safe from all corruption was the Garden of Eden before the Fall.

These images are from life, but processed by memory so that what is unwelcome has been censored. Twain would not have been taken in by another's nostalgia, but his own backward glance is increasingly sacred. It is all that the planet offers that he values. To the tragic losses life has dealt him he has the added folly of his own foolish example, a buccaneer among buccaneers. People disgust him. The blackness of his despair can only be relieved by the play of his imagination. In these brief, infrequent moments he recovers the illusion of his lost self-image. It is radiant with expectations. Life is a movable feast. He walks the length of the table, sampling, describing, confident that there is more where all of that has come from.

Whitman's appetite for life never faltered, being a seamless part of his self-image, but Twain increasingly suffered the torment of the public clown in a private hell. To give expression to his despair preoccupied the last decade of his life. *The Mysterious Stranger* is a remarkable book, and might be read and praised if by another author. Suppose we should hear from God himself that life is a joke? Through the eyes of boys, innocent as God (Twain) has made them, the reader will come to experience the mature judgment of the author. The landscape is a pastoral idyll, fully stocked with everything but people. One day in the woods the boys met a youth who had the powers of creation, and identified himself as an angel named Satan. He was a monstrously clever magician: he knew everything and he had forgotten nothing. He could do no wrong because he had no notion of what it was. One day he explained to the boys, "Life itself is only a vision, a dream. Nothing exists; all is a dream."

"It is true, that which I have revealed to you; there is no God, no universe, no human race, no earthly life, no heaven, no hell. It is all a dream—a grotesque and foolish dream. Nothing exists but you. And you are but a *thought*—a vagrant thought, a useless thought, a homeless thought, wandering forlorn among the empty eternities!"

This book of ultimate, scandalous truth, like *Huck Finn*, is for incurably youthful readers. It is also the anguished cry from the heart of a man exiled from what he holds most dearly—the image he had made of his boyhood. *The Mysterious Stranger* is a boy's revenge on a world that has failed to live up to his expectations. Modern Huck Finns might well read this fable without a pause in their consumption of popcorn and candy. Little of it would prove to be shocking, or rated P.G. Twain passionately hoped to write a book that would horrify his own adult reading public (Mencken's term "Boobocracy" would have delighted him), but the book is notable for its lyrical evocation of an imaginary kingdom where boys could live, roam and never grow up. To the widow of a childhood friend he wrote:

> I should like to call back Will Bowen & John Garth & the others, & live the life, and be as we were, & make holiday until 15, then all drown together.

Huck Finn, Tom Sawyer and the narrating "I" of *The Mysterious Stranger* are all short of fifteen, the date that marked the death of the heart and the corruption of the world. As with Whitman, the crucial image-making was the self-image. He will differ from Whitman in that the period of celebration will prove to be not his manhood but his boyhood, with the exception of the brief hour of fulfillment when he is a cub steamboat pilot on the river. Spells of relief will come as he attempts to salvage, through the eyes of Tom Sawyer and Huck Finn, the receding world of boyhood, but even with Huck he senses that the freedom Huck seeks is an illusion, a "dream" that merely aggravates the condition of slavery. Adults impinge on Huck's world as comical grotesques who exist merely to torment boys or bamboozle and swindle each other. With the exception of the black slave Jim, who arouses both Huck's and Twain's compassion, they are caricatures.

Images of boyhood reflected in the river, at a safe remove from the life along the shores, out of time and out of reach of the long arm of Aunt Sally, celebrate the heavenly cosmos of Sam Clemens. "You feel mighty free and easy and comfortable on a raft" when you recall what it was like some thirty-five years later.

> Sometimes we'd have that whole river all to ourselves for the longest time. Yonder was the banks and the islands, across the water; and maybe a spark—which was a candle in a cabin window—and sometimes on the water you could see a spark or two—on a raft or a scow, you know; and maybe you could hear a fiddle or a song coming over from one of them crafts. It's lovely to live on a raft. . . .

The increasingly disillusioned man, seated in a mansion in Hartford, captive in a scenario of his own devising, conjures up that morning of dawning birdsong, where, crouched in the Lord's baptismal waters, he watches the world emerge out of darkness, for the first time. This is the moment of creation that displaces all others.

> . . . Not a sound anywheres—perfectly still—just like the whole world was asleep, only sometimes the bull-frogs a-cluttering, maybe. The first thing to see, looking away over the water, was a kind of dull line—that was the woods on t'other side—you couldn't make nothing else out; then a pale place in the sky; then more paleness, spreading around; then the river softened up away off, and warn't black any more, but gray; you could see little dark spots drifting along ever so far away—trading-scows, and such things; and long black streaks—rafts; sometimes you could hear a sweep screaking; or jumbled-up voices, it was so still, and sounds come so far; and by and by you could see a streak on the water which you know by the look of the streak that there's a snag there in a swift current which breaks on it and makes that streak look that way. . . .

This subtle and experienced reading of the river is not that of a boy on a raft but of a steamboat pilot who had mastered its moods and language. The appeal and persuasion of this image, however, is that we receive it through a boy's believing eyes. To achieve this is a narrative problem: the writer must create the appropriate voice. The voice, in turn, is a question of language: it must appear to be as natural and free of artifice as Huck Finn himself. The apparent artlessness is a triumph of craft that gratifies both the writer and the reader. Man and boy are combined in this telling in a manner that is seamless, and new to literature. What proves to be irresistibly infectious we recognize as the "vernacular," and from this moment forward this will be the fluent, melodious tongue that Whitman called for—a new tongue for the new vistas, the new times, the New World.

Twain had refreshed himself at the fountain of youth by beginning *Life on the Mississippi:* what he saw of it through a boy's eyes he liked, what he saw through a man's eyes repelled him.

> Then we went loafing around town. The stores and houses was most all old, shackly, dried-up frame concerns that hadn't ever been painted; they was set three or four foot above ground on stilts, so as to be out of reach of the water when the river was overflowed. The houses had little gardens around them, but they didn't seem to raise hardly anything in them but jimpson-weeds, and sunflowers, and ash-piles, and old curled-up boots and shoes, and pieces of bottles, and rags, and played-out tinware. . . .
>
> All the stores was along one street. They had white domestic awnings in front, and the country-people hitched their horses to the awning-posts. There was empty dry-goods boxes under the awnings, and loafers roosting on them all day long, whittling them with their Barlow knives; and chawing tobacco, and gaping and yawning and stretching—a mighty ornery lot. They generly had on yellow straw hats most as wide as an umbrella, but didn't wear no coats nor waistcoats; they called one another Bill, and Buck, and Hank, and Joe, and Andy, and talked lazy and drawly, and used considerable many cuss-words. . . .

This is a mighty strange report from Huck Finn, a refugee from Aunt Sally. The boy Huck could not have cared less about the gardens, the ash piles, the played-out tinware and the loafers roosting on the dry-goods boxes, but the grown-up Huck, and the citizen of Hartford, is scandalized by these tobacco-chawing, aimless, useless idlers with their rude speech and backwoods manners. This was a part of Eden the returning Adam was not prepared for. And yet in all of its details, this loutish, inert world is the paradise that Huck and Tom were at home in. The two worlds of Huck Finn and Mark Twain are at war, and the book fails to reconcile this dilemma. Huck on his raft is in Eden, but on shore it is the unrelieved and lacerating comedy of desperation.

> They swarmed up towards Sherburn's house, a-whooping and raging like Injuns, and everything had to clear the way or get run over and tromped to mush, and it was awful to see. Children was heeling it ahead of the mob, screaming and trying to get out of the way; and every window along the way was full of women's heads, and there was nigger boys in every tree, and bucks and wenches looking over every fence; and as soon as the mob would get nearly to them they would break and skaddle back out of reach. Lots of the women and girls was crying and taking on, scared most to death.

This is a cartoon bedlam, combining elements of Mack Sennett, *Li'l Abner* and other grotesques of frontier humor. But in the past this thronging and hooting mob would have been led by the boy who now observes it with the detachment of an outsider. Huck Finn-Clemens, now living in exile, is appalled by what he sees but feels obliged to admit it. Eden has no place for grownups: they oppress and corrupt. This profound schism in the author's soul cracks the mirrored idyll of a boy and the river. He must continue to float: there is no longer a safe place to land. That second look Twain had had at life along the Mississippi had revealed a corrupted Eden, urgently requiring that he salvage as much of the original as possible. Huck Finn on the raft is that restoration. What he finds along the shores he never really much cared for, as he said himself.

There are moments when the eyes of the author strike a balance with those of the boy Huck Finn, recording a picture that is true in fact as well as fiction.

> Phelps's was one of these little one-horse cotton plantations, and they all look alike. A rail fence round a two-acre yard; a stile made out of logs sawed off and up-ended in steps, like barrels of a different length, to climb over the fence with, and for the women to stand on when they are going to jump onto a horse; some sickly grass-patches in the big yard, but mostly it was bare and smooth, like an old hat with the nap rubbed off. . . .

These details are observed by the author, even as they are processed by the boy's memory. In images of this type, the particulars noted, casually and lyrically strung together, we have the beginning of twentieth-century fiction, with its scrupulous regard for facts and artifacts. The scene is *photographed*, in the care that each detail receives in the recital, and refers us back to Twain's use of the word "snapshot" in his autobiographical comments. Photographs were being taken and published, and they would not have escaped the eye of this original image-maker.

The inventory of the one-horse plantation continues:

> . . . one little hut all by itself away down against the back fence, and some outbuildings down a piece the other side; ash-hopper and big kettle to bile soap in by the little hut; bench by the kitchen door, with bucket of water and a gourd; hound asleep there in the sun; more hounds asleep round about; about three shade trees away off in a corner; some currant bushes and gooseberry bushes in one place by the fence; outside of the fence a garden and watermelon patch; then the cotton fields begin; and after the fields the woods.

This item-by-item scanning, and the use of the semicolon, calls to mind Whitman's snapshot sketches of Broadway, and the writer's eye for the facts. In Twain, however, we sense the writer's preference for the past, rather than the poet's "Democratic Vistas."

> ... The face of the water, in time, became a wonderful book—a book that was a dead language to the uneducated passenger, but which told its mind to me without reserve. . . .

There is an enchantment to be found in early, untrained experience that is gone, forever, from adult experience. Twain accepts this as part of the pain of growing up. That knowledgeable experience might offer something more, something possibly superior, Twain rejects. It will never, he feels, result in *enchantment*. It will never restore the great expectations. In this perspective, growing up is the downward path to wisdom. Nothing will match the dawn of creation observed by the boy seated in the river's shallow water. Curiously, this bitter knowledge, plucked from the tree of life, gives rise to the aftertaste we know as nostalgia. The present may not be so good, but the past was very heaven. Thanks to memory, and imagination, Mark Twain will henceforth have a choice as to where he chooses to live: in the mansion he has built for his bride in Hartford, or in the realm of his imagination.

Part steamboat, part medieval fortress, part cuckoo clock, in part defying description, the Twain mansion in Hartford featured nineteen rooms, five bathrooms, a forest of chimneys, three octagonal turrets (one more than fifty feet high), the exterior ornamented with tile and gingerbread gothic, the interior opulent, the mantelpiece carved with cherubs, gargoyles, sphinxes, griffins, and separate from the house, on a hillside, a private study that resembled a pilothouse. He has just published a novel, *The Gilded Age* (with C. D. Warner), concerned with rampant individualism and unscrupulous speculation of the boom years of the post Civil War, and the emergence of unbridled acquisitiveness. He has also begun his lifelong speculation in inventions, cures and publishing ventures to supply him with the money necessary to his new life. Even as he sits in his pilothouse writing, the present and the future of the nation are taking on their greedy, gilded aspect.

As he writes, he is also increasingly uncertain if his books are for adults or children. He needs an editor's opinion to reassure him. He is captivated—as Huck Finn would be—with the semi-automated house of the millionaire Winans, a museum of inventions and prophetic gadgets. As he writes, he writes less well, and the self-images proliferate. He is at once the humorist and public entertainer, seeking to recover his speculative losses, and the boy from Hannibal, Missouri, seeking to repossess a private garden of delights.

> I remember the pigeon seasons, when the birds would come in millions and cover the trees and by their weight break down the branches. They were clubbed to death with sticks; guns were not necessary and were not used. I remember the squirrel hunts, and prairie-chicken hunts, and wild-turkey hunts, and all that; and how we turned out, mornings, and while it was still dark, to go on these expeditions, and how chilly and dismal it was, and how often I regretted that I was well enough to go. . . . But presently the gray dawn stole over the world, the birds piped up, then the sun rose and poured light and comfort all around, everything was fresh and dewy and fragrant, and life was a boon again. . . .

In numberless echoed versions this idyll of creation will solace the readers whose talents, whose greed, whose expectations find them at the dark end of the acquisitive tunnel, with their eyes riveted rearward on the imagined past. It will be made visible to millions through the illustrations of Norman Rockwell. In this new dispensation it will be possible—as it should be in such an extraordinary country—to experience the exhilaration of the robber baron followed by redemption through nostalgia.

After reading a chapter of *Life on the Mississippi*, in the *Atlantic*, John Hay wrote the author:

> . . . I don't see how you do it. I knew all that, every word of it— passed as much time on the levee as you ever did, knew the same crowd, saw the same scenes—but I could not have remembered one word of it all. You have the two greatest gifts of a writer, memory and imagination.

Indeed he had, and these faculties were in full flower when applied to the romance of his life, the river and the idyll he had made of his boyhood. Only fifteen years younger than Melville and Whitman, Mark Twain felt he was actually present at the creation and had lived to see its imminent destruction. Had Whitman known what Twain's personal life was like, he would have thought him mad. In his seventy years he embraced the world of the noble and not so noble savage, as well as that of the *nouveau riche* and ever-short-of-money speculator. These polarities generated much of his fiction. Perhaps only such a fall from grace as he had experienced would have given him a glimpse of the flawed Eden at the heart of Huck's world. Not Melville's insights and moral passion, or Whitman's sunny fraternal optimism, as he sauntered down the open road of great expectations, but a judgment of life in which a boy's world is repossessed by a man. The garden of delights is limited to male juveniles under fifteen.

At the time Twain was dictating his autobiography, the only escape from the present available to him, Henry James had sailed from England to visit his homeland after an exile of twenty years. The shock of this recognition will be published, a few years later, in *The American Scene*. To a friend, he wrote, "I have need of all your indulgence, feeling, as I do, like a poor helpless baby in the midst of monstrous things."

In *The American Scene* we discover a country that neither Twain nor Whitman appeared to be aware of—the country of the mind. Quantity both preoccupied and gratified Whitman, as quality both puzzled and eluded Twain; only in the mind of James did these flat images overlap to provide a depth of field, a spectrum of revelations. Thanks to his exile, James is the first to "stand right fronting and face to face" to the new century of progress. He will be challenged in such a way as to disturb his composure and enlarge his craft. The spectacle frankly appalls him, but we feel that he finally turns from it with a sense of loss.

# Henry James

The aspect the power wears then is indescribable; it is the power of the most extravagant of cities, rejoicing, as with the voice of the morning, in its might, its fortune, its unsurpassable conditions, and imparting to every object and element, to the motion and expression of every floating, hurrying, panting thing, to the throb of ferries and tugs, to the plash of waves and the play of winds and the glint of lights and the shrill of whistles and the quality and authority of breeze-borne cries—all, practically, a diffused, wasted clamour of *detonations*—something of its sharp free accent and, above all, of its sovereign sense of being "backed" and able to back. The universal *applied* passion struck me as shining unprecedentedly out of the composition; in the bigness and bravery and insolence, especially, of everything that rushed and shrieked; in the air as of a great intricate frenzied dance, half merry, half desperate, or at least half defiant, performed on the huge watery floor. . . .

Nothing James has seen before has brought him to this strident pitch. "The universal applied passion," "the bigness, bravery and insolence," arouses him to a shrillness comparable to what he describes. Fifty years have so congested Whitman's "composition" that "the blab of the pave, tires of carts, sluff of boot-soles," and so on, is a confused "clamour of detonations." This is the aspect of power, and he finds it indescribable.

43

If it *exists*, for James, it will prove to be multifaceted. But such congested tableaux are not congenial to him, since they scramble precisely what he would distinguish.

> . . . I must dip into these depths, if it prove possible, later on; let me content myself for the moment with remembering how from the first, on all such ground, my thought went straight to poor great wonder-working Émile Zola and *his* love of the human aggregation, the artificial microcosm, which had to spend itself on great shops, great businesses, great "apartment houses," of inferior, of mere Parisian scale. His image, it seemed to me, really asked for compassion. . . .

A suitable image for *this* conglomerate is lacking, and James is both put on and put off by it. The view from the Brooklyn ferry, awesome as it might be, was precisely the spectacle that James found wanting, possessing extravagance but lacking intensity. The vast raw mass, heaped skyward, does not draw from James metaphors of natural, or supernatural, constructions, but the thought of what poor wonder-working Zola would do with such abundant resources. He looks on this vast aggregate not as the birth of a colossus but as a numbing aesthetic dilemma. What can one *do* with it? What mystic meaning did this image, on its surface and in its depths, have to give out?

The stereoscope viewer, in vogue at the time, combined two separate images in a manner that a single, three-dimensional image resulted. The multifaceted vision of James sought to combine the numerous overlapping impressions that existed behind every surface. Understandably he was staggered by the kaleidoscopic frenzy of New York. This made for diffusion, not intensity, a swirling disarray of conflicting sensations. James would appear to be the last of all native sons to attempt to come to terms with such disordered impressions. He was held to his purpose by memory and emotion, the need to make a stand on his gathered impressions, but who could have predicted that the master's style would lend itself to what appeared to be so alien? The meandering James sentence, with its snaglike punctuation, grew out of the need to gather a *total* impression, now tripping forward, now tilting sideward, or pausing to take a step rearward, graphically indicating, as in an artist's mock-up, the complications of a full-scale portrait. Only the Jamesian parenthesis will fully respond to the surface and the depth of such a writer's impression, and the knowledge that it is falsified by closure. It must be open to the glance, the hunch, the intuition that he will have as he is writing, and makes him reluctant to pause for longer than a semicolon. "Let me content myself—" he says, but that, happily, will prove impossible. In the prism of Jamesian sensibility the new rich give off endless vibrations.

> . . . The ample villas, in their full dress, planted each on its little square of brightly-green carpet, and as with their stiff skirts pulled well down, eyed each other, at short range, from head to foot; while the open road, the chariots, the buggies, the motors, the pedestrians—which last number, indeed, was remarkably small—regarded at their ease both this reciprocity and the parties to it. It was in fact all *one* participation, with an effect deterrent to those ingenuities, or perhaps indeed rather to those commonplaces, of conjecture produced in general by the outward show of the fortunate life. That, precisely, appeared the answer to the question of manners: the fact that in such conditions there couldn't *be* any manners to speak of; that the basis of privacy was somehow wanting for them; and that nothing, accordingly, no image, no presumption of constituted relations, possibilities, amenities, in the social, the domestic order, was inwardly projected. . . .

This is just such an utterance, we are free to guess, that might have stirred Mr. Dooley to implore James to "spit it up in Papa's hand." The play of light on the scene does much to obscure it: the refracted impressions leave the observer blinking. Nor does "perhaps indeed rather" provide the pause that enables the reader to get his bearings. This is not darkest James, the subject being elementary, but we see why the best book on an immense subject is also the one least read. The *kernel* of this many-faceted impression follows a page later:

.... The highest luxury of all, the supremely expensive thing, is constituted privacy—and yet it was the supremely expensive thing that the good people had supposed themselves to be getting. . . .

That is luminous James—but the reader might be nodding, or blinking, at the moment this light flashes. The vigilance required to follow James is in accord with the intensity of his vibrations, but it is not always in phase with the reader's capacities. The mind must either be nimble or be dazzled and aggravated.

. . . There was the oddity—the place was furnished by its own good taste; its bosky ring shut it in, the two or three gaps of the old forgotten enclosure made symmetrical doors, the sweet old stones had the surface of grey velvet, and the scattered wild apples were like figures in the carpet.

This is so right, and so characteristic, we recognize the hand of the painter in this single stroke. The image is sophisticated, audacious and exactly right to the point he is making. An elegance in the commonest of objects, the simple landscape furnished by its own good taste. The bad taste is imminent with the entrance of a pair of summer girls, and a summer youth:

. . . The freedoms of the young three—who were, by the way, not in their earliest bloom either—were thus bandied in the void of the gorgeous valley without even a consciousness of its shriller, its recording echoes. The whole phenomenon was documentary; it started, for the restless analyst, innumerable questions, amid which he felt himself sink beyond his depth. The immodesty was too colossal to be anything but innocence—yet the innocence, on the other hand, was too colossal to be anything but inane. And they were alive, the slightly stale three: they talked, they laughed, they sang, they shrieked, they romped, they scaled the pinnacle of publicity and perched on it flapping their wings; whereby they were shown in possession of many of the movements of life.

What *were* the freedoms of the young three? James has perfectly described his own flustered response, but he has failed to communicate what caused it. We know only that the liberties bandied in the void leave the mother serene, and the other passengers unperturbed. We can guess that what took place was the flirtatious horseplay of the male and female of the species on a summer outing. It is, indeed, inane, but it is also common to the country he has returned to. *The manners, the manners,* of which James is a supreme master, vibrate so strongly in the presence of native display he fails to see what is obvious. The relatively inane do have their freedoms, and they have been from the first the customs of the country from which he has veiled his eyes. *Manners* should have spared James his sense of troubled exposure—as he spared himself in his fiction—otherwise he is roused to note with approval that they are in possession of "the movements of life."

Jamesian snobbery, as essential to his nature as the large liberty of summer to the young three, provided the ground for his perception. Although his taste is affronted, his intelligence perceives the loss of *conscious* life in such an exhibition, a loss so common it would soon pass for consciousness.

> No impression so promptly assaults the arriving visitor of the United States as that of the overwhelming preponderance, wherever he turns and twists, of the unmitigated "business man" face, ranging through its various possibilities, its extraordinary actualities, of intensity. . . . Nothing, meanwhile, is more concomitantly striking than the fact that the women, over the land—allowing for every element of exception—appear to be of a markedly finer texture than the men, and that one of the liveliest signs of this difference is precisely in their less narrowly specialized, their less commercialized, distinctly more generalized, physiognomic character.

Having stretched the canvas, James applies the color:

> The right kind of woman for the American man may really be, of course, as things are turning out with him, the woman as to whom his most workable relation is to support her and bear with her—just as the right kind of man for the American woman may really be the man who intervenes in her life only by occult, by barely divinable, by practically disavowed courses. . . . It in any

case remains vivid that American life may, as regards much of its manifestation, fall upon the earnest view as a society of women "located" in a world of men, which is so different a matter from a collection of men of the world; the men supplying, as it were, all the canvas, and the women all the embroidery.

This analysis anticipates the numerous novels men will write in the next half-century, as well as the fiction the liberated woman now contributes to this subject.

Without *manners*, it has been suggested, the American novelist is without a subject larger than his own self-centered impressions. This defines a concept of the novel rather than a concept of the novelist. In a world without manners we feel that James would have learned, as others have learned, to write fiction. The mind that is fertilized by the virus of suggestion is subject to the large liberty of image-making, and the results are inspired fiction whether in or out of the novel.

> The moral in question, the high interest of the tale, is that you are in the presence of a revelation of the possibilities of the hotel—for which the American spirit has found so unprecedented a use and a value . . . and making it so, at this supreme pitch, a synonym for civilization, for the capture of conceived manners themselves, that one is verily tempted to ask if the hotel-spirit may not just *be* the American spirit most seeking and finding itself. . . .

> It sat there, it walked and talked, and ate and drank, and listened and danced to music, and otherwise revelled and roamed, and bought and sold, and came and went there, all on its own splendid terms and with an encompassing material splendour, a wealth and variety of constituted picture and background, that might well feed it with the finest illusions about itself. . . . One was in the presence, as never before, of a realized ideal and of that child-like rush of surrender to it and clutch at it which one was so repeatedly to recognize, in America, as the note of the supremely gregarious state. It made the whole vision unforgettable, and I am now carried back to it, I confess, in musing hours, as to one of my few glimpses of perfect human felicity.

In a context of non-fiction, this is matchless fiction, the "it" evoking a neutered faceless image, an anonymous presence, free of the burden of constituted privacy. The ache of envy James feels at what he beholds will be shared by the majority of his readers, since there are few Americans who have not tasted of this experience. Opulence, euphoria and that dream of dreams, an immense and protected promiscuity that carries everything before it.

Although James was all for full consciousness, for writer and reader to be one on whom nothing is lost, he was increasingly aware of the cost of such attention to the conscience and the burden of such knowledge to the artist. In the preface to *What Maisie Knew* he wrote:

> . . . Successfully to resist (to resist, that is, the strain of observation and the assault of experience) what would that be, on the part of so young a person, but to remain fresh, and still fresh, and to have even a freshness to communicate?

Style is that element in his writing over which the writer has the least control. It will prove to be present at those moments the writer mimics or parodies another writer (as in Hemingway's parody of Anderson) and believes himself to be free of this self in his act of impersonation. The style of James invites parody, but resists imitation. In the samples I have quoted, he departs from the detached tone of his fiction, and the relatively straighter line of narration, for the freedom of movement and range appropriate to his subject. His eye must be free to follow his impressions, and the words free to follow his eye. The familiar shibboleths of a "good style," directness, simplicity, economy, and so on, appear to be deliberately excluded. To follow the bouncing ball of his imagination, the incisive glimpses of his intuition, is an exhilarating challenge to the writer and he shares this adventure with the reader.

Nothing like this had confronted James before, and there is nothing remotely like his response. Density, intensity, prolixity commingle in page after page, chapter after chapter, and will go far to explain why *The American Scene* is known to readers, if at all, in fragments, such as those I have been quoting. It may be a book destined to persist through hearsay,

> The cold passed reluctantly from the earth, and the retiring fogs revealed an army stretched out on the hills, resting.

As Hemingway said, it was plain to see this boy had never seen a *real* war. It is all writing. Images of his non-fevered imagination. He had read a few books. As Balboa had gazed at the Pacific, Crane had looked into the Civil War photographs of Brady. A real war would not have suited his talents so well, being a soldier's war rather than an author's. Since he was only twenty-two years of age, he needed the perspective provided by history. He perceives the confusions of his own war clearly, with the irony and pathos of a survivor. A real war, as he discovered later, would never have resulted in *The Red Badge of Courage*. For all of his obsession with the "facts" of real life, he intuited the primacy of the imagination. As his imagination cools, the facts will prove to mean less and less.

The characteristic labor pains of creation are not part of his talent. This makes him a difficult object of study. He has obsessions. He roams about awaiting inspiration. For a few brief years he has the gift of imagery, he is a maker of signs. This faculty is common to those who visualize, carve idols, paint walls or create masks, but it is unusual in a young man with a talent for words. He has to gesture with words. Do not weep, he says, war is kind.

He is so often a painter, with an eye for color, we might ask why he does it with words.

> In the swirling rain that came at dusk the broad avenue glistened with that deep bluish tint which is so widely condemned when it is put into pictures. There were long rows of shops, whose fronts shone with full, golden light. Here and there, from drug-gists' windows or from the red street-lamps that indicated the positions of fire-alarm boxes, a flare of uncertain, wavering crimson was thrown upon the wet pavements.

We see that he is familiar with Impressionist painting, but he prefers stronger contrasts.

> . . . A river, amber-tinted in the shadow of its banks, purled at the army's feet; and at night, when the stream had become of a

sorrowful blackness, one could see across it the red, eyelike gleam of hostile camp-fires set in the low brows of distant hills.

In the cadence of the line, whether long or short, we have the sense of extreme deliberation in the choice of words.

> . . . The moon had been lighted and hung in a treetop. The liquid stillness of the night enveloping him made him feel a vast pity for himself.

This is the antithesis of James, where parenthesis leaves all options open. Crane appears to describe a scene that is already captured, and awaits recording. The right word, to his context, is the audacious word. The celebrated example of the image as a symbol is:

> The red sun was pasted in the sky like a wafer.

This was first written as a *fierce* wafer. In the end he preferred it with the fierce deleted, a matter of the ear correcting the eye. He is our first *modern* writer in his obsession with appearances. His telling images combine photographic exactness with impersonal appraisal.

> Once the line encountered the body of a dead soldier. He lay upon his back staring at the sky. He was dressed in an awkward suit of yellowish brown. The youth could see that the soles of his shoes had been worn to the thinness of writing paper, and from the great rent in one the dead foot projected piteously. And it was as if fate had betrayed the soldier. In death it exposed to his enemies that poverty which in life he had perhaps concealed from his friends.

This is at once real and surreal. A matchless fictive distance, made possible by the voice, makes the impersonal comments natural and moving. He is able to impose on what appears to be the facts what is most personal to the writer.

> I understand [he wrote] that a man is born into the world with his own pair of eyes and he is not at all responsible for his vision— he is merely responsible for his quality of personal honesty.

We might ask how a youth so wise ripens into wisdom. The

ironic is so natural to his mode of feeling that he is free of cynicism. In a chapter deleted from the final manuscript we have this brief revelation of youthful ardor:

> It was always clear to Fleming that he was entirely different from other men, that he had been cast in a unique mold. Also, he regarded his sufferings as peculiar and unprecedented. No man ever achieved such misery. There was a melancholy grandeur in the isolation of his experiences.

Irony so dominates this complaint the effect is that of self-parody. The suffering youth mocks his suffering. The perspective on experience it takes decades to acquire he slipped into, and out of, in a brief season. The perfect expression of all that he had mastered is compressed into the tale of "The Open Boat." A ship is wrecked, and the men are adrift at sea. The knowledge that they might drown has made them reflective.

> ... Other people had drowned at sea since galleys swarmed with painted sails, but still—
>
> When it occurs to a man that nature does not regard him as important, and that she feels she would not maim the universe by disposing of him, he at first wishes to throw bricks at the temple, and he hates deeply the fact that there are no bricks and no temples. . . .
>
> A high cold star on a winter's night is the word he feels that she says to him. Thereafter he knows the pathos of his situation.

This pathos is scrutinized through the "soldier of the legion who lay dying in Algiers," a line of sentimental verse that he had previously failed to appreciate. It proves to provide a measurable intrusion, in a scene of shipwreck, but so masterfully done that the reader is persuaded to share this pathos and delay the story.

Thomas Beer has guessed that "the mistress of this boy's mind is fear." It is too neat a formula, but the line might have been taken from *The Red Badge of Courage* as a clue to its hero, and gives it a resonance that is haunting. Is it fear, as in the example of Hemingway, that compels him to test the grain of his nature, seeking out wars, revolutions and shipwrecks?

Paradoxically, his eyewitness experience of war lacks the power of the war he totally imagined. He may have found it a disordered, secondhand experience, lacking the coherence of good fiction. What was there further to be won from war than the profound pathos of his situation? What else had it to teach him he felt no compulsion to learn?

"The Open Boat," a long tale intended to be after the fact, is the summit of Crane's achievement. Since we have the factual report of the same incident, it provides an unexampled illustration of the role of imagination in great fiction. Crane is almost morbidly scrupulous to observe all the facts. Once they have been determined, he is able to possess them in imaginative terms. In the large sense, the change is one of expansion— a recital of facts is fleshed out into fiction—but the freedom of consequence to the tale is Crane's identification with all the elements. No other occasion, in his brief creative life, provided him with materials that were so congenial. The sea, the open boat, the flickering prospect of the shore were image symbols to which he could give the full charge of his emotions. In *The Red Badge of Courage* he had created the style which had awaited on this further level of involvement. Crane's personal war with the elements is in the open boat.

> None of them knew the colour of the sky. Their eyes glanced level, and were fastened upon the waves that swept toward them. These waves were of the hue of slate, save for the tops, which were of foaming white, and all of the men knew the colours of the sea. The horizon narrowed and widened, and dipped and rose, and at all times its edge was jagged with waves that seemed thrust up in points like rocks.

The tautness of this language is like that of ropes holding a full sail. It holds the reader to its purpose, and compels him to reflect on what he is reading. The cadence is hypnotic, and actually discourages a clear impression of what is occurring. It seems real enough, but it is all illusion, with waves that are barbarously abrupt and tall. The day is so somber, whatever its color, it seems too grave for ironic comment. One of the men tries to steer with a little thin oar, and the correspondent pulls at the other and wonders why he is there.

> In the wan light the faces of the men must have been grey. Their eyes must have glinted in strange ways as they gazed steadily astern.

This problematic comment wonderfully enhances the impersonal forces the men are facing.

> ... Viewed from a balcony, the whole thing would doubtless have been weirdly picturesque. But the men in the boat had no time to see it, and if they had had leisure, there were other things to occupy their minds. The sun swung steadily up the sky, and they knew it was broad day because the colour of the sea changed from slate to emerald green streaked with amber lights, and the foam was like tumbling snow. The process of the breaking day was unknown to them. They were aware only of this effect upon the colours of the waves that rolled toward them.

In this tale of the sea it all comes together, with a style to match the complexity of Crane's emotions and to challenge him to present them as true to the facts. In it, without intrusion, he comes to terms with the "abiding pathos of his situation," but it will prove to be the nature of this catharsis to leave him with diminished motivations. That might well be the only irony to escape his observation. For the imaginary soldier who lay dying in Algiers he now feels a profound and impersonal comprehension—by his own definition this is the summit of man's otherwise pathetic situation. Here was an actuality that was at once stern, mournful and fine.

With the achievement of this story the creative tension in Crane's nature relaxes. That is my guess. He continues to work, but with less brilliance, and there is much in his new fame as a writer to distract him. He is famous: he is always in need of money: he has a wife and the friendship of Joseph Conrad.

Crane is not the first to write about life before he has experienced much of it at first hand, but he is a pioneer in his respect for facts while the possessor of an imagination of genius. This circumstance made him acutely aware of what has come to be an American dilemma—a distrust of what is loosely called fiction, and an obsession with what appears to be the facts. Crane had no mind to ponder the metaphysics of it, or distinguish between the current and popular labels applied to the novel, but he keenly felt the urgency of a new sensibility. He was as conscious of his intent to make it new as Joyce or Pound. "The Bride Comes to Yellow Sky" and "The Blue Hotel" are images that evoke the colors of van Gogh and look ahead to the show of Fauve painting held three years after his death. As a painter, he would have been one of the century's prophets: as a writer, an *American* writer, his imagery merely seemed bizarre.

A man adrift on a slim spar
A horizon smaller than the rim of a bottle
Tented waves rearing lashy dark points
The near whine of froth in circles.
                    God is cold.

The puff of a coat imprisoning air:
A face kissing the water-death
A weary slow sway of a lost hand
And the sea, the moving sea, the sea.
                    God is cold.

These incisive images are sign and symbol of Crane's appraisal of man's condition. The sea, the sea, is all around us. God is cold. Only a great and ponderable terror earns the soul the privilege of facing such facts. This still-young man was equally blended of fire and ice.

# Willa Cather

The meeting of Cather and Stephen Crane, in Lincoln, Nebraska, in the spring of 1895, as unlikely as "The Bride Comes to Yellow Sky," and as visually memorable as "The Blue Hotel," is one of the few star-crossed moments in American letters. Crane was twenty-four, Cather twenty-two, but in the meeting we can sense her assurance in being on her home ground. The famed author of *The Red Badge of Courage* was on his way to Mexico. One oppressively hot night he talked to Cather within the sound of "the twang of banjos" from the lower veranda of the Hotel Lincoln. "He spoke slowly, even calmly, but I have never known so bitter a heart in any man as he revealed to me that night."

For a young man to reveal such a bitter heart he may have had his needs, as well as his motives. We can assume she made a perfect listener for his dim view of the world. "The detail of a thing," he told her, getting down to essentials, "has to filter through my blood, and then it comes out like a native product, but it takes forever." His listener would never receive more seminal advice.

At that time Crane had but five short years to live, and felt the urgency of those whom the gods love to get his work done. This meeting of youthful minds on a sultry plains night is an image both memorable and haunting. What a pity the grain of his remarkable nature did not lend itself to the bittersweet nuances of romance, the story of a lonely correspondent caught between trains on the sealike plains. How did he see this young woman who heard so well all that he said, and much that he did not?

Whatever Stephen Crane may have thought of the world, he was very much of his time and place. Willa Cather, born in Virginia, was very much at home in pioneer Nebraska, but as progress and business interests took hold the frontier virtues receded. What had been the right place was proving to be the wrong time. The belief that one is born at the wrong time, and in the wrong place, is common to imaginative people. In the teeming throngs of the modern city all mannner of men and women, from all parts of the planet, appear to be part of the same decade, but in their eyes and their obsessions we know they do their living elsewhere. Willa Cather realized early that she was out of place in the twentieth century.

On a visit to her brother, in the Southwest, she had her first glimpse into the world of the Ancient People, the canyons and cliff dwellings of the Pueblo Indians. The Indian had shaped this world with his hands, and it had shaped him. More to her point, the hand of the potter, the water-carrier, proved to be that of a woman.

> On the first day that Thea climbed the water-trail, she began to have intuitions about the women who had worn the path, and who had spent so great a part of their lives going up and down it. She found herself trying to walk as they must have walked, with a feeling in her feet and knees and loins which she had never known before . . .

In the example of the Pueblo people she found the perfect symbol of "constituted privacy," so crucial to her nature, and the timeless elements of civilized existence. They, too, had cut themselves off from surrounding dangers in order to cultivate their own gardens, and the "images" of dwelling, painting, weaving and dancing derived from the interplay of man, woman and nature. Cather is obstinately organic where she

intuits what it is that matters. She recognized in this drama of
man and nature the rock on which to build her own fictions.

As a rule, it is men, not women, who extol the virtues of
pioneer hardships, the confrontation with the elements, the
attractions of an inhospitable landscape. The treeless wind-
swept plains, the unlimited horizon, a frozen sea of whiteness
in the winter, perhaps a plague of grasshoppers in the summer,
were the despair of most women but prefigure, for Cather, the
durable nature of the human drama. Not pioneer hardship but
civilized progress, the westward course of the business empire,
chilled her heart.

Two years after her first glimpse of the Ancient People she
published *Song of the Lark*. It is the least satisfactory of her
novels (as she knew) but it is of interest in the way it
foreshadows the emerging writer. She explicitly tells us that
her purpose was to give a portrait of the young artist: Thomas
Mann had done this in "Tonio Kröger" and Joyce in his
*Portrait of the Artist as a Young Man*. Cather's effort was not
of this order, but she shared with the writers of her time a
common impulse and hunger. She also felt the stirrings of an
additional concern, the portrait of the artist as a young
woman.

> "Suppose," Fred came out at length—"suppose I were to offer
> you what most of the young men I know would offer a girl they'd
> been sitting up nights about: a comfortable flat in Chicago, a
> summer camp up in the woods, musical evenings, and a family to
> bring up. Would it look attractive to you?"
>
> Thea sat up straight and stared at him in alarm, glared into his
> eyes.
>
> "Perfectly hideous!" she exclaimed.
>
> Fred dropped back against the old stonework and laughed deep
> in his chest.
>
> "Well, don't be frightened. I won't offer them. You're not a
> nest building bird. You know I always liked your song, 'Me for the
> jolt of the breakers!' I understand."
>
> She rose impatiently and walked to the edge of the cliff. "It's
> not that so much. It's waking up every morning with the feeling
> that your life is your own, and your strength is your own, and

your talent is your own; that you're all there, and there's no sag in you."

This avowal is made ten years before *The Professor's House,* where the professor, St. Peter, has his study in the attic. Occasionally it is shared with a dressmaker, and the "forms" that are used in dressmaking.

These "forms" were the subject of much banter between them. The one which Augusta called "the bust" stood in the darkest corner of the room, upon a high wooden chest in which blankets and winter wraps were yearly stored. It was a headless, armless female torso, covered with strong black cotton, and so richly developed in the part for which it was named that the Professor once explained to Augusta how, in calling it so, she followed a natural law of language, termed, for convenience, metonymy. Augusta enjoyed the Professor when he was *risqué,* since she was sure of his ultimate delicacy. Though this figure looked so ample and billowy (as if you might lay your head upon its deep-breathing softness and rest safe forever), if you touched it you suffered a severe shock, no matter how many times you had touched it before. It presented the most unsympathetic surface imaginable. Its hardness was not that of wood, which responds to concussion with living vibration and is stimulating to the hand, nor that of felt, which drinks something from the fingers. It was a dead, opaque, lumpy solidity, like chunks of putty, or tightly packed sawdust—very disappointing to the tactile sense, yet somehow always fooling you again.

The meaning of this explicitly symbolic "form" is so plain and unvarnished the reader blinks. One knows that it is Cather, as well as the Professor, who rejects the role of the female as child-breeder and home comforter in all of its ironic implications. The age of Mother-power, anticipated by Lardner, has not yet clouded the public horizon, but Cather is intimate with its nature, and in this quick portrait hoped to put it behind her.

The seeds of Thea Kronborg's experience with the cliff-dwellers, mystical in nature, and the landscape of the vanished Ancient People were ten years, and four novels, in coming to full maturation. Tom Outland intrudes on the Professor's orderly life, and his story intrudes on Cather's novel. The Professor and Tom Outland each experience a life of early promise and emerging disenchantment, but Outland's story, a primal vision of an earthly Eden, of lost innocence and heart's desire, so moves and captivates the reader that the Professor and his problems are forgotten. Outland has breathed the air that gives life, the Professor has breathed the air that impaired it. This contrast did not work to the advantage of the novel, but it enhanced the world of the Blue Mesa. Cather felt the urgency, and the truth, of two stories: the life-enhancing experience of Tom Outland, the life-depleting experience of the Professor. Tom Outland's vision is the one that captures the reader:

> The cabin stood in a little grove of piñons, about thirty yards back from the Cruzados river, facing south and sheltered on the north by a low hill. The grama grass grew right up to the door-step, and the rabbits were running about and the grasshoppers hitting the door when we pulled up and looked at the place. There was no litter around, it was clean as a prairie-dog's house. . . . A-long the river the cottonwoods and quaking asps had already turned gold. Just across from us, overhanging us, indeed, stood the mesa, a pile of purple rock, all broken out with red sumach and yellow aspens up in the high crevices of the cliff. From the cabin, night and day, you could hear the river, where it made a bend round the foot of the mesa and churned over the rocks. It was the sort of place a man would like to stay in forever.

Shortly later, Outland stumbles on the evidence of early human habitation.

> To people off alone, as we were, there is something stirring about finding evidences of human labour and care in the soil of an empty country. It comes to you as a sort of message, makes you feel differently about the ground you walk over every day.

Cather had felt that difference in every fiber of her nature, and she is eager to share it with the reader.

> . . . The bluish rock and the sun-tanned grass, under the unusual

purple-grey of the sky, gave the whole valley a very soft colour, lavender and pale gold, so that the occasional cedars growing beside the boulders looked black that morning. It may have been the hint of snow in the air, but it seemed to me that I had never breathed in anything that tasted so pure as the air in that valley. It made my mouth and nostrils smart like charged water, seemed to go to my head a little and produce a kind of exaltation. I kept telling myself that it was very different from the air on the other side of the river, though that was pure and uncontaminated enough.

When Outland discovers the cliff dwelling, it is the tower that holds his eye, and is the focus of Cather's mounting emotion:

It was beautifully proportioned, that tower, swelling out to a larger girth a little above the base, then growing slender again. There was something symmetrical and powerful about the swell of the masonry. The tower was the fine thing that held all the jumble of houses together and made them mean something. It was red in colour, even on that grey day. In sunlight it was the colour of winter oak-leaves. A fringe of cedars grew along the edge of the cavern, like a garden. They were the only living things. Such silence and stillness and repose—immortal repose. That village sat looking down into the canyon with the calmness of eternity. The falling snow-flakes, sprinkling the piñons, gave it a special kind of solemnity. I can't describe it. It was more like sculpture than anything else. I knew at once that I had come upon the city of some extinct civilization, hidden away in this inaccessible mesa for centuries, preserved in the dry air and almost perpetual sunlight like a fly in amber, guarded by the cliffs and the river and the desert.

For a moment he ponders if he should intrude upon this place, or keep it the way the mesa had kept it, inviolate as a tomb. His decision to share it will prove fatal. The cliff city will lose its treasure to a museum collector, and Outland will lose the friend he had trusted. At the close of his adventure he knows the cliff city has given him his moments of greatest fulfillment.

... Something had happened in me that made it possible for me to co-ordinate and simplify, and that process, going on in my mind, brought with it great happiness. It was possession. The excitement of my first discovery was a very pale feeling compared to this one. For me the mesa was no longer an adventure, but a religious emotion. . . .

Happiness is something one can't explain. You must take my word for it. Troubles enough came afterward, but there was that summer, high and blue, a life in itself.

Happiness for Willa Cather was the shared emotion of discovery and reverence for the cliff city. As this experience recedes, happiness recedes and a growing discontent emerges. The nature of this discontent, with civilization and its ways, is revealed in the Professor's house. Compared with what Tom Outland had experienced on the Blue Mesa, the Professor felt himself to be cheated, to have surrendered what he should have cherished.

He loved his family, he would make any sacrifice for them, but just now he couldn't live with them. He must be alone. That was more necessary to him than anything had ever been, more necessary, even, than his marriage had been in his vehement youth.

Reflecting back on his life, he recalls his boyhood in Kansas:

... the Professor felt that life with this Kansas boy, as little as there had been of it, was the realest of his lives, and that all the years between had been accidental and ordered from outside. . . .

The Kansas boy . . . was a primitive. He was only interested in earth and woods and water. Wherever sun sunned and rain rained and snow snowed, wherever life sprouted and decayed, places were alike to him. . . . He seemed to be at the root of the matter; Desire under all desires, Truth under all truths.

There is no mistaking the personal accent of this passage. It is not so bitter, but it is of the same substance as Mark Twain's cry of anguish, to "be as we were, & make holiday until 15, then all drown together."

Blighted great expectations is an American specialty. Time would increase Cather's discontent, her sense of alienation within her own culture, as the vision of Tom Outland receded into the reaches of Panther Cañon. The shallowness and vulgarity of the "business" culture, with its bitch goddess Success, did not arouse her to ridicule or satirize it as it did Mencken and Sinclair Lewis. Its effect on Cather was that of a blight she must escape. In this circumstance she turned again to her own cherished landscape, but in another century. *Death Comes for the Archbishop* provides her with the stretch of canvas to paint on, and arouses her to moments of rapture, of blissful transport, comparable to her experience at the Blue Mesa.

> His first consciousness was a sense of the light dry wind blowing in through the windows, with the fragrance of hot sun and sagebrush and sweet clover; a wind that made one's body feel light and one's heart cry, "Today, today," like a child's. . . . Something soft and wild and free, something that whispered to the ear on the pillow, lightened the heart, softly, softly picked the lock, slid the bolts, and released the prisoned spirit of man into the wind, into the blue and gold, into the morning, into the morning!

This description of the spirit's release from confinement is as explicit as words will allow. We know how profoundly it speaks for Cather. In such a landscape the creations of nature sometimes prefigure the images of imagination. The Archbishop beholds, in a singular juniper, that "living vegetations could not present more faithfully the form of the cross."

To this writer, relationship with a place, a chosen place, takes precedence over relationships with people. The spirit of place is the larger spirit, and it is that place that will endure. The Great Good Place of her imagination was the Southwest, with the Blue Mesa on the horizon, a moment in time when man and nature lived in a life-enhancing communion, no matter how difficult. The rock on which she would build is exemplified in Catholic feeling, traditions and continuity, but if we look behind this façade, into the shadows of her novel, we find the elements of order that were part of her childhood

in Virginia. Those years that are missing from her fiction—
even her reflections on the nature of fiction—provided the
substructure and the disposition necessary to her experience of
life on the frontier, in the Southwest and in the parish.

In the years of her discontent one book was published that I
believe would have restored her flagging spirits: *The Wife of
Martin Guerre,* by Janet Lewis, a tale of sixteenth-century
France, evokes as words seldom can what is timeless, what is
unchanging, in the interplay of nature with human passions.
The flowering imagination, rooted in the earth, projects a
landscape that resists erosion, inhabited by people whose
likeness to the startled reader is a never-ending source of
wonder.

It is of interest to me, personally, that Cather came to the
plains at the age of nine, the year that I left them. My own
childhood provided me with little in the way of conscious
observation, but a sufficiency of the ingrained disposition for
the life and the landscape. A few years later, a small-town boy
in Chicago, I would experience the first tantalizing vicarious
glimpses of the West I came too late for, and must therefore
re-create. In American experience this ingrained disposition
will generate countless imaginary landscapes, each with the
hallmark of the writer. Cather's Blue Mesa, Crane's Blue
Hotel, Hemingway's Two-Hearted River, Faulkner's Yoknapa-
tawpha County. An early severing of such umbilical ties often
proves to be helpful in their eventual replacement with the ties
of fiction, immaterial images that resist erosion.

# Gertrude Stein

Few centuries have presented so many bizarre faces to the future as the one that opened with Crane's death in London. Gertrude and Leo Stein were living on the Rue de Fleurus, in Paris, where they briefly shared and nurtured two of the century's transcendent egos.

> Both were dressed in chestnut-colored corduroy, wearing sandals after the fashion of Raymond Duncan, whose friends they were. Too intelligent to care about ridicule, too sure of themselves to bother about what other people thought, they were rich and he wanted to paint.

The idyll is troubled by a shift of the ego center to the massive, Roman-headed Gertrude. Forces are stirring in her that trouble Leo.

> Slowly and in a way it was not astonishing but slowly I was knowing that I was a genius and it was happening and I did not say anything but I was almost ready to begin something.

Compared with his sister, Leo Stein's egotism was self-absorbing and superficial. Slowly and in a way astonishing she was knowing that she was a genius. Thanks to Leo, she had read Flaubert, and applied herself to a translation of his *Trois Contes*. The first of these tales, "A Simple Heart," concerns a

profoundly simple soul, Félicité, servant to Madame Aubain
for half a century.

> She had had her love-story like another.
> Her father, a mason, had been killed by falling off some
> scaffolding. Then her mother died, her sisters scattered, and a
> farmer took her in and employed her, while she was still quite
> little, to herd the cows at pasture. She shivered in rags and would
> lie flat on the ground to drink water from the ponds; she was
> beaten for nothing, and finally turned out for the theft of a
> shilling which she did not steal.

The inarticulate soul, the seemingly artless style, the flow of
events in the timeless present so approximate the nature of
"The Good Anna" we can appreciate the author's shock of
recognition.

> You see that Anna led an arduous and troubled life.
> The good Anna was a small, spare, German woman, at this time
> about forty years of age. Her face was worn, her cheeks were thin,
> her mouth drawn and firm, her light blue eyes were very bright.
> Sometimes they were full of lightning and sometimes full of
> humour, but they were always sharp and clear.

The life is simple, the words are simple but the mind of the
writer is complex. The presence of the writer in the narrating
voice is seldom apparent, and never intrusive.

> Anna found her place with large, abundant women, for such
> were always lazy, careless or all helpless, and so the burden of
> their lives could fall on Anna, and give her just content. Anna's
> superiors must be always these large helpless women, or be men,
> for none others could give themselves to be so comfortable and
> free.

Gertrude Stein speaks of her debt to Cézanne, from whom
she learned, she says, that all the parts of the picture are equal,
there are no incidental or subordinate portions; and this effect
can be seen in what she has written. The writer explicitly
maintains an immediate present, in which the relevant elements make their appearance.

> Anna looked very well this day. She was always careful in her dress and sparing of new clothes. She made herself always fulfill her own ideal of how a girl should look when she took her Sundays out. Anna knew so well the kind of ugliness appropriate to each rank in life.

The manner in which Stein is invisibly present in this portrait is masterly. The good Anna is far from the Rue de Fleurus, the paintings of Cézanne and the aesthetic discussions of Stein and her brother Leo, but once Stein had tapped her Baltimore experience she is the source, in her own words, of a syrup that flows. Occasionally, what she had learned from William James forces her hand to "psychological" insights.

> In friendship, power always has its downward curve. One's strength to manage rises always higher until there comes a time one does not win, and though one may not really lose, still from the time victory is not sure, one's power slowly ceases to be strong.

This is self-evident in the good Anna's experience, but the writer is moved to underline it. The perfection of tone in Anna's story is subtly complicated by her German accent, although we are spared the usual dialect. It is apparent in the slight twists of syntax:

> A sad disgrace did once happen in the family.

and the accumulation of adjectives:

> Old Katy was a heavy, ugly, short and rough old German woman. . . .

Although a vernacular American sentence, it has the heavy weight of German sentiment behind it, suggesting an accurate translation. Children would seem to be congenial to this picture—the voice and tone are those often affected in stories for children—but these housebound women, large and small, are not absorbed with the rites of reproduction. The sentiments usually reserved for children are shared with dogs.

> The good Anna had high ideals for canine chastity and discipline. The three regular dogs, the three that always lived with

Anna, Peter and old Baby, and the fluffy little Rags, who was always jumping into the air just to show that he was happy, together with the transients . . . were all under strict orders never to be bad one with the other.

"One with the other" rings a change on the familiar "with one another." Stein is on record as saying that these innovations held no conscious interest for her, but a mind of such complexity does not *naturally* fall into the language and rhythms of simplistic narration.

You see that Anna led an arduous and troubled life.

is as explicitly artful as Crane's

He held a little carnival of joy on horseback.

Both want an image that captures the complexity of emotion. Stein seeks to mirror the fluid, shifting surface of consciousness. In her own fashion, however, she proposes to be one on whom nothing of the *interior* life is lost. She had received from William James the germinal suggestion that consciousness was a "stream" of sensations, and she knew that an image of consciousness should reinforce this perception. In the story "Melanctha" the flow and repetition are carried as far as the tone of narration will permit.

Why did the subtle, intelligent, attractive, half white girl Melanctha Herbert love and do for and demean herself in service to this coarse, decent, sullen, ordinary, black childish Rose, and why was this unmoral, promiscuous, shiftless Rose married, and that's not so common either, to a good man of the negroes, while Melanctha with her white blood and attraction and her desire for a right position had not yet been really married?

Limited exposure, at the right time and place, is more favorable to the imagination than a long, familiarizing saturation, which ends in dulling the first impressions. The Negro talk that Stein heard while she lived in Baltimore, and the lives she observed, perfectly mirrored the flow of consciousness much more than white talk, with its cultivated mannerisms and inhibitions. The vagaries, deviations and artful repetitions accurately imaged the stream of emotions below the surface. With this writer the feeling was paramount, and from the feeling flowed the relevant impressions; the transcendent imaginative gift was in the power she exercised to be the *other*. Enhancing her already matchless assurance is Stein's fully conscious awareness of being a woman—one of the first to give the measure of womanly feeling. The good Anna, the gentle Lena, the tormented Melanctha are possessed and revealed in such a manner we feel only a woman might have achieved it. That is a hazardous presumption—the world is peopled with women shaped by male imaginations—but Gertrude Stein might well be the first to free herself of prior, man-fashioned examples. In this achievement the oceanic depths of her ego provided the necessary ballast. Her immense self-assurance spares the reader the special pleading of the liberated woman, a posture she would have found demeaning. As we see her in Davidson's massive sculpture, and Picasso's portrait, she exists like a force of nature. Having looked around, she needed to do no more than look within.

> Sometimes the thought of how all her world was made, filled the complex, desiring Melanctha with despair. She wondered, often, how she could go on living when she was so blue.

The more pronounced and innovative a writer's style, the more self-limiting it often will prove to be. One Melanctha is unique, a technical and imaginative triumph, but a second character in this manner would suggest a parody of the original. This dilemma exists within the story itself, where other characters are cut from the same fabric. Their endless discourse dissolves palpable distinctions, which would seem to be part of the author's purpose.

> After all, to me one human being is as important as another human being, and you might say that the landscape has the same values, a blade of grass has the same value as a tree. Because the realism of the people who did realism before was a realism of trying to make people real. I was not interested in making the

people real but in the essence or, as a painter would call it, value.

The writer who is prone to theorize, like Stein, is not always a good judge of what the writer has written. The good Anna and Melanctha are clearly distinct as people, as well as values. D. H. Lawrence had a similar intuition which was contradicted by his practice.

> You mustn't look in my novel for the old stable *ego* of the character. There is another ego, according to whose action the individual is unrecognizable, and passes through, as it were, allotropic states which it needs a deeper sense than any we've been used to exercise, to discover are states of the same radically unchanged element.

There *is* another ego, as Lawrence has perceived, but it should not and does not keep us from recognizing the old stable ego in his fiction. Fiction is about people, stable and unstable egos, and the impression we receive that these people are real.

For all the remarkable diversity of their individual talents, a mania "to make it new" seemed to possess the more ambitious of the turn-of-the-century talents. Stein's ambition, as she has told us, was second to none. In Paris she had the example of numerous painters of genius. The innovations of Cézanne, Picasso and the Cubists had more influence on her talent than what her contemporaries were writing. For one thing, pictures could be *looked* at; books required reading. What she had learned in her first, apprentice-size novel, she would apply to a project in the grand manner. "The grand manner" would appear to be the one thing she accepted from male practice. Proust, Joyce and Mann provided examples she could appreciate without reading.

> . . . In trying to make a history of the world [*her* project] my idea here was to write the life of every individual who could possibly live on the earth. I hoped to realize that ambition. My intention was to cover every possible variety of human type in it. I made endless diagrams of every human being, watching people from windows and so on until I could put down every type of

human being that could be on the earth. I wanted each one to
have the same value.

For a novelist, that is remarkably explicit. *The Making of
Americans* begins like this:

> It has always seemed to me a rare privilege, this, of being an
> American, a real American, one whose tradition it has taken
> scarcely sixty years to create. We need only realize our parents,
> remember our grandparents and know ourselves and our history is
> complete.

No obsession with *roots* from this creator of a new world. It
is also uncharacteristically straightforward, the tone suggestive
of an earnest commencement speaker. Thirty pages later she is
warming to her larger subject, which is still herself:

> . . . Yes I am strong to declare that I have it here in the heart of
> this high, aspiring, excitement loving people who despise it
> [Paris],—I throw myself open to the public,—I take a simple
> intererst in the ordinary kind of families, histories, I believe in
> simple middle class monotonous tradition, in a way in honest
> enough business methods.

Another one we know was strong to declare it, and also
threw himself open to the public, if not in Paris.

These are really the thoughts of all men in all ages and lands, they
    are not original with me,
If they are not yours as much as mine they are nothing, or next to
    nothing.

No one in Paris seemed aware that this extraordinary
woman, a gifted writer and collector of paintings, held such a
high opinion of the middle class, their monotonous tradition
and honest enough business methods. Appropriately she
evokes, in one short sentence, the sentiment and syntax of Walt
Whitman, that lover of the bulk people in all lands. More to his
point, we see the crucial role that the new American language
plays and will play in the making of Americans, and American
writers.

Middle-class, middle-class, I know no one of my friends who will admit it, one can find no one among you all to belong to it . . . and yet I am strong, and I am right, and I know it, and I say it to you and you are to listen to it, yes here in the heart of a people who despise it. . . .

Such passages, regrettably, are seldom quoted, hardly being congenial to the avant-garde reader with a taste for Stein. Therewith, and plain enough to understand it, is the new democratic vista as seen from the Rue de Fleurus. In affirmation and assurance it matches Whitman. She is strong, she is right and she knows it. Every vernacular syllable attests to it. This darling of the innovators, the intellectual élite, sits relaxed in the kitchen of the good Anna, the better to hear of the sad disgrace that did once happen in the family. She has spoken plainly so we know exactly where she stands.

. . . but only certain men and women, and the children they had in them, to make many generations for them, will fill up this history for us of a family and its progress.

These words have music, a cadenced insistent repetition, and a complexity of meaning that is unique. She knows what a novel is, and it is no mistake that she calls what she is doing a history. That leaves her free to do it her own way, and anticipate the predictable criticism. What is her own way? She allows herself space and time to warm up.

In the summer it was good for generous sweating to help the men make the hay into bales for its preserving and it was well for one's growing to eat radishes pulled with the black earth sticking to them and to chew the mustard and find roots with all kinds of funny flavors in them, and to fill one's hat with fruit and sit on the dry plowed ground and eat and think and sleep and read and dream and never hear them when they would be calling. . . .

That seems a strange pastoral idyll for the girl from Oakland, California, and the young scholar from Baltimore, Maryland, currently very much at home on the Rue de Fleurus in Paris. It belongs on the same shelf as *Huck Finn,* but bound in the same blue cloth as Aunt Sally. We are still close to the cadence of *Three Lives,* and such characteristic twists as "when they would be calling," giving the lilt of a ballad to "monotonous tradition."

If we can speak of a core to Stein's concept of consciousness, it would lie in the nature of repetition. Ceaseless repetition, with minimal gradual changes, like the wash of water on a beach. In the abstract it is simple, and can be simply stated. As it manifests itself in life, however, in consciousness, it is ceaselessly, inexhaustibly self-creating and self-modifying. Stein has peered into the oceanic depths of this rhythm, and she is captivated and obsessed with what she sees. She cannot look long and long enough. She cannot repeat it often and often enough.

> Every one then has a history in them by the repeating that comes out from them. There are some who will have sometime the whole repeating of each one they have around them, they will have the whole history of each one, there is repeating then always in every one, there is repeating always of the kinds of all women and men. There is repeating then always in every one; that makes a history of each one always coming out of them. There is always repeating in every one but such repeating always has in it a little changing . . . the whole repeating that comes out from them every one who has living in them, the whole repeating then in them and coming out from each one is a whole history of each one.

In the traditional craft of fiction this one paragraph would suffice for the whole. By repeating she illustrates what is meant by repeating. The student of fiction would underline the repeated words, the echoing rhythms, and the word would get around among the *cognoscenti* that this woman loved and practiced repetition. In *The Making of Americans,* however, this is how all Americans are made. Several hundred pages, perhaps a hundred thousand words, are devoted to the nuances of repetition insofar as they can be captured in words. It is the reluctance of language to deal with her impressions, her intuitions, that compels the writer to write as she does, since she knows what she knows and she will not be diverted.

Complaints of automatic writing are bound to occur in such a tidelike repeating of what has been repeated, a backing and filling, a swelling and decreasing, with only minimal palpable changes. I am persuaded she knows what she is doing, and she does it (allowing for the amplitude of her demonstration), but a problem lies with the reader. Repetition is also lulling, stupefying, numbing and mind-drugging, inducing a state of consciousness that is largely non-conscious. As much as half of this book might be chanted by the young, and old, as mantras. Since this manuscript was completed in 1908 and not published until 1925, the heat of creation cannot be given as an excuse for the length of her demonstration. Her book is considerably longer than *Ulysses*, but not so long as À *la Recherche du Temps Perdu*. We may have a clue to its length in the fact that large books would soon become synonymous with large talents, and no large talent was more self-assured than Stein's. If it would take a large book to establish her genius, here was a large book. We know that Hemingway briefly assisted in its preparation for publication, and that a close reading of this remarkable prose made upon him an indelible impression. And well it might.

> . . . This is one then, I will now describe others of this family of kinds in men and women, for soon now I will describe Alfred Hersland for I am completely always nearer understanding that one and yet there are some difficulties that I am still feeling and I am very full up now with this kind of them the Alfred Hersland kind of them and still I am feeling some difficulties in the completion, they are not yet to me all of them entirely completely yet whole ones inside me, I am waiting and I am not yet certain, I am not yet impatient yet in waiting, I am waiting, I am not now again beginning, I do not feel that I need to be again beginning, I am in the right direction, I am only now just needing to be going, I am now only just waiting, I am going I think very soon to be keeping on going. . . .

If a spiritualist had the gift for and the need of incantation, I think this might do. Shades are called upon to indicate they are present. In the psychological and spiritual torment there is a hint of almost physical labor. In the self-exhortation there is much of Henry James's *"Causons, causons, mon bon!"* appeal to his genius. It is no accident that both writers were committed to the *expansion* of consciousness, American consciousness standing in desperate need of such expansion. If we compare this passage to one in *Three Lives*, we see how far, and how little, the writer has come in her effort to *image* repetition. The familiar external ties have dissolved, and it is now more depth psychology than fiction, a pumping at the source with verbal priming, an effort to heave up, to throw up, as in a flow of lava, the abiding forces below the surface.

> I could go on and on, I am so certain that it would be a very important thing if some other going on being living, some other ones going on being in living could be knowing really how to be distinguishing the resisting from the attacking kind in men and women, could be understanding the way having it in them to have religion in them is in them of the resisting kind of them, is in them of the attacking kind of them. I am so certain that I am knowing a very great deal about being being in men and in women that it certainly does seem as if something would be missing if not any one would be coming to know from me all of that everything.

If we are reading, if we are still reading, this passage is in no way unusual. At long and long last we have been shaped to her purpose. This is surely the way the mind slips, slides, twists and turns, peaks and hollows, as it pulses and breathes like the sea's surface.

> . . . I could though be so wise and I am so wise and it would be so nice for me to be certain that from me some other one could be a wise one a little less wise than I am who am the original wise one. . . . I am almost certain I am completely a wise one. I will not tell any more now about this thing. I will tell now some more about religion and about attacking and about resisting being and I will tell some more now about everything and perhaps sometime I will be sad again about not any one ever having the understanding of being in men and women that I am having.

Seated at her feet we nod in agreement. Yes you are you are

you are the original wise one. You do go on and on and on, but you are the wise one, and your vast incantation is both a séance and a book of wisdom, a ceaseless probing of what is hesitantly conscious, a deliberate rejection of what is reasonably lucid, a supplement to Henry James, a parallel to *Finnegans Wake,* being a womanly version of the keys to, given, the riverrun from swerve of shore to bend of bay is no longer past Eve but *through* her, this commodius vicus of recirculation bringing us back to the point of departure, almost.

> Every one then is an individual being. Every one is like many others always living, there are many ways of thinking of every one, this is now a description of all of them. There must then be a whole history of each one of them. There must then now be a description of all repeating. Now I will tell all the meaning to me in repeating, the loving there is in repeating.

Traces of Madame Sosostris and Madame Blavatsky can be seen in her performance. The paradox in her method is that the ceaseless repeating diminishes, rather than enhances, the individual being. *Being* an individual, the reader wearies. He is engulfed in this lapping of water music. What a great pity it is that the good decent middle class, in a way honest enough in their business methods, from which has always sprung the best the world can offer, finds it unreadable.

# Sherwood Anderson

How significant words had become to me. At about this time an American woman living in Paris—Miss Gertrude Stein—had published a book called *Tender Buttons* and it had come into my hands. How it had excited me. Here was something purely experimental and dealing in words separated from sense—in the ordinary meaning of the word sense—an approach I was sure the poets must often be compelled to make. Was it an approach that would help me? I decided to try it.

Sherwood Anderson was not in exile. He had not lived in England, like James and Crane; he had not lived in Paris, like Gertrude Stein. He had not actually *lived* in New York. He had lived in Camden, Clyde and Elyria, Ohio, before going to Chicago. This ascending lisp, from the small town to the big one, had been of minor consequence to previous American writers, but it was to be the prototype for the next generation.

At the beginning of the long twilight of a summer evening, Sam McPherson, a tall big-boned boy of thirteen, with brown hair, black eyes, and an amusing little habit of tilting his chin in the air as he walked, came upon the station platform of the little corn-shipping town of Caxton in Iowa.

This invokes a ceremony of innocence that openly appeals to the reader. It is simple in style, and simple in intent, lacking

the complexity of Stein's syntax. The long twilights of the
Midwest summer evenings contain the larger part of Anderson's nature. The day passes that this long twilight might
begin. At its approach the writer is drawn from the house, the
store or the office where he is idling, to walk down the shaded
streets to the open country that surrounds the small town.

Every man, and in particular every American, wants to tell
you his life story. Every man, and in particular Sherwood
Anderson, wants to explain himself.

> As I write this I am remembering that my father, like myself,
> could never be singly himself but must always be playing some
> role, everlasting-strutting on the stage of life in some part not his
> own.

Is that true? Anderson is not scrupulous about his facts. His
public image is a soft-focus portrait of the artist as a middle-
aged bohemian, a pose derived from his reading. The smoldering leaf-burning fires of adolescence are at the heart of
Anderson's pastoral idyll. The reluctance he felt toward growing up, and out, is linked to the depth of this backward
longing. The long, long twilight of the summer evenings
encompasses the vagaries, the yearnings, the great expectations
that both generate and stifle consciousness. Anderson is at one
with this life, but he lacked Stein's knowledge and sophistication. The burden of America's new wisdom is the expanding
consciousness of adolescence, and literature is its re-enactment.
Anderson hesitated to free himself of the illusions that gave
him the greatest comfort. He wrote: "It must be that I am an
incurable small town man," a prospect that pleased him. In the
emerging identity sweepstakes it reassured him as to who he
was. It nurtured the fiction that he would write about himself.
He was not a small-town man, but neither was he at home long
in Chicago or New York, or at ease in London or Stein's Paris.
If we ponder where Anderson might prove to be at home, we
have the example and figure of Whitman. Both men are on
the move: they are part of the throng of the open road.
Anderson is a small-town man if we grant that *all* small towns

are his province. These are the golden harvest years of the tramp and the hobo, the new breed of subculture hero, their campfires visible far down the tracks of any small town located on a railroad. They were the first to give their troubled but alluring endorsement to the option of *flight*.

In the middle of his life, thirty-seven years of age, finding himself in the dark wood of the business jungle, Anderson wrote a note to his wife, spoke to his secretary and was last seen, hobo-fashion, walking down the tracks toward an unknown destination. In such a manner was born the archetypal figure who walks away from his past (the *walk* was important, the railroad tracks an assured direction) into a challenging self-fulfilling future. Since that man was Anderson, it is little wonder that he found it hard to distinguish, in his actual life, between facts and fiction. To the image of the long twilights of summer we add the image of real and imagined escape. Windy McPherson's son Sam was a rough, untutored portrait of the author. He writes this book in Chicago, the terminus of his flight, looking backward to ponder what it was that made him a "truth seeker." At the end of this novel he has found a new life, nevertheless:

> A shudder ran through his body and he had the impulse to run away into the darkness, to begin again, seeking, seeking.

Sam McPherson resists, but Anderson will continue to find the allure of seeking irresistible.

How did a businessman in Elyria, Ohio, persuade himself that he was a "truth seeker"? It is a naïve term for a man of his age, but it truthfully suggests his confused state of mind. Was he seeking something, or was he fleeing something? The artist is a finder, not a seeker, but the seeker is the more romantic figure. He questions, he sits brooding, he searches within himself for elusive answers. To the first postwar decade of the twentieth century this proved to be an appealing role. The Old World, too, is rife with truth seekers who are asking, and answering, what it is to be an artist. In Munich Thomas Mann puts the question to Tonio Kröger, and in Trieste an Irishman in exile puts it to himself. Among these subtle and disciplined truth seekers Sherwood Anderson is the naïve. He wants to say, and say again, "What is the grass?" But it has been said. He is enchanted by a seeker like Gertrude Stein, but essentially ignorant of what she has found. Both Stein and Anderson anticipate the guru that lurks in the depths of the American psyche, eternally awaiting resurrection, but the naïve artist was spared the need to make fundamental distinctions. The impersonal voice, an imaginative triumph in Crane's "The Open Boat," and Stein's *Three Lives*, gives way to the personal admission:

> Mother was tall and slender and had once been beautiful. She had been a bound girl in a farmer's family when she married father, the improvident young dandy. There was Italian blood in her veins and her origin was something of a mystery. Perhaps we never cared to solve it—wanted it to remain a mystery. It is so wonderfully comforting to think of one's mother as a dark beautiful and somewhat mysterious woman.

This is part of his storyteller's story. His mother had not been a bound girl, and his father was not an improvident dandy. Nor was there in his mother's veins Italian blood.

To distinguish between his *own* voice, self-evident in this excerpt, and the impersonal voice of the imagination will remain, for Anderson, a seldom long resolved dilemma. The language for this voice he had at hand:

> Upon the half decayed veranda of a small frame house that stood near the edge of a ravine near the town of Winesburg, Ohio, a fat little old man walked nervously up and down. Across a long field that had been seeded for clover but that had produced only a dense crop of yellow mustard weeds, he could see the public highway along which went a wagon filled with berry pickers returning from the fields.

The vocabulary is as simple as that of *Three Lives*, and relatively free of snagging punctuation. We sense that the lines are deliberately extended to enhance the desired impression. The author has not intruded into the story, and the reader is at ease with the narrator's distance. It is a story about hands, the nervous expressive hands of Wing Biddlebaum.

No one had made such a point about hands in just this way. Or about "Paper Pills," or "Godliness," or "Loneliness"— images that seemed to trap the lives they suggested. Living in Chicago, but still full of Winesburg, Ohio, as Stein had been full of Baltimore, Anderson had achieved the "distance" that excluded the anxious, hovering author. It is a brief triumph, controlled yet revealing, an original American blend of craft sophistication and naïveté. The author is forty years of age. Both he and the time are ripe. In the two years between "Hands" and "The Book of the Grotesque," he has mastered the voice necessary to his impressions.

> The writer, an old man with a white moustache, had some difficulty in getting into bed. The windows of the house in which he lived were high and he wanted to look at the trees when he awoke in the morning. A carpenter came to fix the bed so that it would be on a level with the window.

This is flawless. The image is free of intrusion and self-indulgence. The imaginative act of being the *other* has come to him without effort, and needs no elaboration. What he has to tell us, strange as it sounds, is that people who believed they possessed a truth became grotesques.

> It was the truths that made the people grotesques. The old man had quite an elaborate theory concerning the matter. It was his notion that the moment one of the people took one of the truths to himself, called it his truth, and tried to live his life by it, he became a grotesque and the truth he embraced became a falsehood.

This is a great and healing wisdom for one who began as a "truth seeker." We can also understand how appreciative Gertrude Stein would have been of this knowledge.

> You can see for yourself how the old man, who had spent all of his life writing and was filled with words, would write hundreds of pages concerning this matter. The subject would become so big in his mind that he himself would be in danger of becoming a

grotesque. . . . It was the young thing inside him that saved the old man.

That is a second and less dramatic truth, but not so easily resolved as he suggests. This subject does, indeed, become big in him, and he will never long be free of its presence and the voice created to express it. It is an alluring, balladlike music that has awaited, it would seem, for this strolling player to sing it. Other writers are quick to lend an ear to it, to imitate or ridicule it, but will seldom long be free of its spell. The secret of this spell lies in the emerging language itself. Those who rigorously shape it, like Stephen Crane, do not release the flood tide of its promise as openly, as prodigally, as the storyteller from Elyria, Ohio. In his opinion not only writers of genius but every man has a story to tell, and the language to tell it.

From Whitman through Crane, Stein, Anderson, Lardner, Hemingway and Faulkner, it is the language that has possessed the writer, and spoken through him more than he consciously willed or intended. This has its price, and those deepest in debt continue to pay it.

> . . . His was that fumbling for exactitude [Faulkner writes of Anderson], the exact word and phrase within the limited scope of a vocabulary controlled and even repressed by what was in him almost a fetish for simplicity, to milk them both dry, to seek always to penetrate to thought's uttermost end. He worked so hard at this it finally became just style. . . .

So it did for most of them, including the writer of this passage. The individual writer is a perceptible ripple in the vast current of language that bears him seaward as the flood bears the topsoil, and its cargo of flotsam, "the bitter apple and the bite in the apple." Occasionally it flatters the writer with the notion that he, not the language, is the master of what he surveys. Hemingway will pick up, right where Stein put it down, the language that exhausts the writer to the extent he believes he owns it. Anderson seeks to free himself of the story about himself:

Besides, I shall tell the tale as though you, my readers, were personal friends. We are walking together, let's say on a country road. The road follows a stream and the day is pleasant. We are unhurried. We stop at times to sit on rocks beside the stream. We arise and walk again and I talk.

One thing leads to another as he walks and talks, as he talks and walks, through the eternal twilight of the summer evening that captivates his imagination.

I keep talking, love to talk. I am telling you that this thing happened to me, that thing happened.

He is full of himself, this writer, and like a child he is eager to share it. More of a seeker than a finder, more of a loser than a winner, basking in the words and phrases that fill the crannies and kinks of the mind like water, a sensuous, caressing creature comfort of melodious sounds, mouth-filling vowels, into which we dip our faces and drink.

Yesterday morning I arose at daybreak and went for a walk. There was a heavy fog and I lost myself in it. I went down into the plains and returned to the hills, and everywhere the fog was as a wall before me. Out of it trees sprang suddenly, grotesquely, as in a city street late at night people come suddenly out of the darkness into the circle of light under a street lamp.

The walker lost in the fog, absorbed with his impressions. The images that recur to his imagination. Trippers and askers surrounded Whitman wherever he sauntered, or loafed at his ease, but this walker has as his companion only the phantoms of his imagination. Up ahead, where he is gazing, the open road leads back to the lonely crowd.

To Dreiser he wrote:

In your play American Tragedy the play ends by the pronouncement that we can forgive the murderer but that society cannot be forgiven. To tell the truth Ted I think it nonsense to talk this way about society. I doubt if there is any such thing. If there is a betrayal in America I think it is our betrayal of each other.

For the seeker this is one truth he can abide in, and tirelessly share with the phantom listener. His one story seeks to hold the listener until he, in the telling, stumbles on its meaning, his pleasure in the knowledge that in this sharing he has found a truth.

# Ring Lardner

A long solemn-faced man. The face was wonderful. It was a mask. All the time you were with him you kept wondering . . . "What is going on back there?"

On meeting Lardner in 1933, Anderson recorded this impression.

Much that was going on back there could be read in the daily Chicago *Tribune*, where Lardner had his own column. He reported on what he saw and heard around him, with emphasis on what he heard. The medley of utterance, not necessarily speech, that constituted the American vernacular was in full flower. Lardner had been a sportswriter, with an entrée into the palmy world of baseball. The inwardly tormented, outwardly disfigured, brooding and groping grotesques of Anderson's imagination were also the kith, kin and kissing cousins of the loud-mouthed, horseplaying, four-flushing bush leaguers just emerging from the dark woodwork of rural and small-town life. The country hick was on his way to becoming the big-city slicker. A gap once too broad for leaping separated Winesburg, Ohio, from the ball park in Detroit or Chicago.

He ast me one time, he says: "What do you call me Ike for? I ain't no Yid."

Humor this broad and slangwich this bad are now part of the new language heralded by Whitman. The most fluent and melodious-voiced people in the world read the new literature while waiting for a haircut.

> I said to Mother: "Well," I said, "I guess it's a good thing every day ain't your birthday or we would be in the poorhouse."
>
> "No," says Mother, "because if everyday was my birthday, I would be old enough by this time to of been in my grave long ago."
>
> You can't get ahead of Mother.

The first American spouse to refer to his wife as "Mother" deserves the monument we erect to fallen heroes. Lardner is the first to spot and identify this native species. Is she "the right kind of woman for the American man . . . and is he the right kind of man for the American woman?"

> Mother says that when I start talking I never know when to stop. But I tell her the only time I get a chance is when she ain't around, so I have to make the most of it. I guess the fact is neither one of us would be welcome in a Quaker meeting, but as I tell Mother, what did God give us tongues for if He didn't want we should use them?

Anderson's characters speak plainly enough, but not often, as if speech cost them much effort. The tone of his writing is oral, and the reader seems to intrude into a discourse that has no end. The monologue or dialogue casually breaks off, to begin again the following morning. This style of narration suited the needs of Lardner's column, as well as the attention span of his readers. A Lardner innovation is the use of quotations to emphasize high points of humor. The images are flat, bold as the cartoons in full bloom in the comic pages. On many occasions the cartoon "balloon" would have served Lardner's purpose better than quotation marks. The refrain "You can't get ahead of Mother" would have served as the title of a serial.

Compared with Lardner's slangy, up-to-the-minute report-ing, Anderson seems the writer of an earlier decade. Lardner appears to dispense with the familiar distinctions between literature and life. People seldom sound as good as he reports them, but they would if they could. He is at ease in the tradition of the journalist-satirist, given authority and appeal by Mark Twain, but he departs from the humorists that preceded him in the cutting edge of his mockery. The sword of his wit gives the *coup de grâce* to Mother, the back of his hand to Father, the flat of the blade to the reader. The uproarious, guffawing surface of the world of "You Know Me, Al" did conceal from Lardner the crassness and vacuity of the life beneath it. Though he was as romantically ready for life as Fitzgerald, the aftertaste of his humor has the bitterness of alum. Like Hemingway, he looked about him and saw a dream corrupted. Increasingly, his humor was that of a man betrayed by the people he had hoped to believe in. In the place of Anderson's brooding grotesques Lardner inserts the caricature, the animated look-alikes shaped by that staple of American life, the wisecrack.

> For one thing he asked me if I had heard Rockefeller's song and I said no and he began singing "Oil alone." Then he asked if I knew the orange juice song and I told him no again and he said it was "Orange juice sorry you made me cry." I was in hysterics before we had been together ten minutes.

"I Can't Breathe," the diary of a teen-ager besieged on her vacation by old and new boyfriends, is one of the most "hysterically" successful of Lardner's acid portraits. This nameless diary writer anticipates the mindless subspecies of Nathanael West and the remarkable juveniles of J. D. Salinger. There is no hint that Lardner's *jeune fille* is acquiring experience, or that the passage of time will result in a larger awareness, or "growth," or that her nature is complex enough to be probed for its "hurt," its numb core of feeling. The humor seems good clean all-American fun until it goes a bit sour as the diary closes. Is she a moron? In the passage of time will the boy she marries refer to her as Mother? The reader is free to assume she will learn no more than how to breathe.

This is one about a brother and sister and the sister's husband and the brother's wife. The sister's name was Rita Mason Johnston; she was married to Stuart Johnston, whose intimates called him Stu, which was appropriate only on special occasions. The brother was Bob Mason, originally and recently from Buchanan, Michigan, and in between whiles a respected resident of Los Angeles. His wife was a woman he had found in San Bernardino and married for some reason.

Whatever effect this had on the readers, it would prove unforgettable on the writers. The concreteness, the economy, the irony are all a seamless part of the language; no cues for laughs are necessary. The closing sentence is a story within a story, at once "humorous" and searingly sarcastic. Nevertheless, the impression persists that it is all there, for free, in the language.

Dear Miss Gillespie: How about our bet now as you bet me I would forget all about you the minute I hit the big town and would never write you a letter. Well girlie it looks like you lose so pay me. Seriously we will call all bets off as I am not the kind that bets on a sure thing and it sure was a sure thing that I would not forget a girlie like you and all that is worrying me is whether it may not be the other way round and you are wondering who this fresh guy is that is writing you this letter. I bet you are so will try and refreshen your memory.

Writers other than Lardner, all readers of Lardner, will create the new conscience of the postwar generation. Lardner's remarkable talent seems to be merely part of the language itself. Not a few readers, reading Lardner, would feel that they should try their hand at writing. How could they miss? All he did was see and hear what was free as the air. Only the writer will perceive that these *images,* so artless-seeming, are matchlessly crafty. He is not always so good. If he had been, a decade of writers would have been silenced. In the easeful achievement of his vernacular style we see ourselves like the reflections in shop windows. How lifelike we are! As a rule, neither so handsome nor so dreadful as we feared. Wheezing with laughter, Lardner's readers are often unaware in what way they are being tickled. Sinclair Lewis will be the first to reap the harvest of "types" that the new public seems prepared for. As a laugh purveyor to a nation of "boobocrats," Lardner was well paid, famous and full of self-loathing. The admiration of critics and writers he admired aggravated his suspicions that he had wasted his talents. The measure of his achievement, however, is not in what the "serious" writers said about him, but in the way they absorbed him, more an act of recognition than plagiarism. He was part of the news that had become part of urban life. Like Twain and Stein, he is invisibly present in the images we have shaped of ourselves, the gargoyles and leering comical "mugs" that small fry paint on the benign, reassuring faces in Norman Rockwell's *Saturday Evening Post* covers.

> "What do you go around in?" inquired his brother-in-law.
> "I've got a 1924 Studebaker," said Bob.
> "No, no," said Stu. "I mean your golf game."

In Lardner's mocking glance there is more of the cutting edge of Swift than the chuckle of Twain. "The laceration of laughter that ceases to amuse" can be heard offstage.

Between vaudeville, the movies, the novels and the horseplay, it was getting harder and harder to recognize *real* life. Americans were long accustomed to laughing at each other: through Lardner they were compelled to laugh at themselves. Laugh shows were on the airwaves, where the roars of laughter, on summer evenings, competed with the sound of the player piano. A narrowing spectrum of "types," Mom and Pop, Harold Teen, the loudmouth, the cornball, the Babbitt, replaced the anonymous cast of individual eccentrics Anderson continued to mull over. Those who had been to war returned to brood about it, or to write about it, or stayed in Europe and swelled the colony of exiles. Others returned to inadvertently discover the "region," the nation's nooks and crannies, the hamlets and hobo jungles, the big and small two-hearted rivers and tobacco roads still to be heard from. The crackling discharge of imaginative energy was as palpable as summer lightning. The euphoria of the twenties bedazzled many, bewildered others, provided space-launching pads for the affluent and the chosen and left upon natives and curious foreigners indelible impressions of the American self-image. Among them, a romantically eager and love-struck bootlegger; an emasculated correspondent, and bullfight observer; a tireless, giant-striding, life devourer and seeker, consumed with his longings; a cultivated lady lost on the plains, with the courage and will to find herself; a real-estate broker in the city of Zenith; an idiot observing the sound and fury of Southern decay. Fitzgerald from St. Paul, Hemingway from Oak Park, Willa Cather from Red Cloud, Sinclair Lewis from Sauk Centre, Tom Wolfe from Asheville, Faulkner from Oxford, Mississippi, Eliot from St. Louis, Pound from Idaho are representative figures in a sunburst of image-makers. Many testified to the singular fact that small towns were often big places to be from. Others to the superstition that once the hometown was left, there was no going back.

In this upsurge of self-awareness, self-fulfillment and self-indulgence, the voice of sanity is often that of a woman. Women are not new to American writing, but they are writing with a new force and assurance. Both Willa Cather and Katherine Anne Porter reflect the example of Flaubert at the moment the vernacular tide is cresting. There is little fiction as good as, and none better than, Janet Lewis's *The Wife of Martin Guerre* and Katherine Anne Porter's *Noon Wine*, examples of the craft of fiction notably free of the male ego as a fearless barrier breaker, freedom fighter and truth seeker.

# T. S. Eliot

... (where every word is at home,
Taking its place to support the others,
The word neither diffident nor ostentatious,
An easy commerce of the old and the new,
The common word exact without vulgarity,
The formal word precise but not pedantic,
The complete consort dancing together)...

—"Little Gidding", T. S. Eliot

These are the fragments shored against the ruins:

A patient etherised upon a table
A life measured out with coffee spoons
Arms that lie along a table, or wrap about a shawl
A pair of ragged claws, scuttling across the sea's floor
An old man in a dry month
A dull head among windy spaces
Fear in a handful of dust
Withered stumps of time
Fingers of leaf that clutch and sink
Bats with baby faces
Garlic and sapphires in the mud
At sea the dawn wind wrinkles and slides

These images, like chips of marble, strew the shores of our
shared imagination. What is it like to read for the first time,

Let us go then, you and I,
When the evening is spread out against the sky
Like a patient etherised upon a table . . .

For audacity of imagery they call to mind Crane's

Tented waves rearing lashy dark points
The near whine of froth in circles.
                        God is cold.

"The common word exact without vulgarity, the formal word precise but not pedantic, the complete consort dancing together." The patient etherized upon the table will prove to be the metaphor for numberless occasions.

No poet seems to be more English and less American. The meter is iambic, far from the tribe's barbaric yawp: the evening is spread out against the sky of London. After the cups, the marmalade, the tea, the women who come and go, talking of Michelangelo, the poet hopes to force the moment to its crisis.

April is the cruellest month, breeding
Lilacs out of the dead land, mixing
Memory and desire, stirring
Dull roots with spring rain.

In neither the lines of *The Waste Land* nor its scholarly apparatus is there an American author. The unreal city is London, the river is the Thames. The tones are inspired by the intuition that words themselves speak louder than the individual poet, being in themselves poems. April, cruellest, lilacs, dead land, memory and desire, roots, spring rain are words that approximate signs, images. Scholars were proving this to be true at the moment that the writers and poets divined it. The common word is as layered with history as Troy. The moment of truth in the cliché awaits on the context that will restore it to usage. Simple words serve complex intentions.

Here I am, an old man in a dry month,
Being read to by a boy, waiting for rain.

But a strange poet, surely, to have come out of St. Louis. Malcolm Cowley expressed a common complaint:

> It was as if he were saying, this time, that our age was prematurely senile and could not even find words of its own in which to bewail its impotence; that it was forever condemned to borrow and patch together the songs of dead poets.

Why, then, this poet's power to capture the imagination?

The images of despair in *Prufrock* and *The Waste Land* reflect the poet's personal anguish: the readers found in these images the metaphor for postwar disillusion, and the emerging landscape of the Depression.

What are the roots that clutch, what branches grow
Out of this stony rubbish? Son of man,
You cannot say, or guess, for you know only
A heap of broken images, where the sun beats,
And the dead tree gives no shelter, the cricket no relief,
And the dry stone no sound of water.

This imagery derives from literature, rather than experience, but it is given new life through the poet's emotion.

For I have known them all already, known them all—
Have known the evenings, mornings, afternoons,
I have measured out my life with coffee spoons . . .

The assured finality of this world-weariness is only possible to a poet, in exile, who is intimate with the best writers. Not in the meter, or the image, but in the exactness of the common word we recognize the poet's ancestry.

The yellow fog that rubs its back upon the window-panes,
The yellow smoke that rubs its muzzle on the window-panes
Licked its tongue into the corners of the evening,
Lingered upon the pools that stand in drains,
Let fall upon its back the soot that falls from chimneys,
Slipped by the terrace, made a sudden leap,
And seeing that it was a soft October night,
Curled once about the house, and fell asleep.

Americans found it hard to reconcile this academic and scholarly poet with the masters of the vernacular. Yet it is this paradox that reassures us as to what is basic in image-making. While the poet waits on the emergence of memory, literature and observation are processed by emotion.

April is the cruellest month

restores to poetic usage a word encrusted with sentiment and clichés. Rebirth is more than reawakening. The audacity of the image is matched by the poet's easy assurance. He knows he is on firm ground. The cadence is liturgical. The voice is that of a chorus burdened with wisdom that must be shared as a prelude to forgiveness. The dialect is that of the tribe, honed and purified. It is the poet's deliberate and didactic intention to echo

Whan that Aprille with his shoures soote
The droghte of March hath perced to the roote

In such a manner his poem is at once traditional, modern and un-American. Like James and Pound, he was determined not to be provincial.

Summer surprised us, coming over the Starnbergersee
With a shower of rain; we stopped in the colonnade,
And went on in sunlight, into the Hofgarten,
And drank coffee, and talked for an hour.

This scan of appearances is cinematic, encompassing experience as movement, movement as experience. The poet assumes that we are familiar with the sensation, need his words only as a reminder.

His father told him that story: his father looked at him through a glass: he had a hairy face.

So Joyce, in a few lines, scans childhood. The words offer clues, in the manner of promptings, acknowledging that the experience lies within the reader.

And when we were children, staying at the archduke's,

My cousin's, he took me out on a sled,
And I was frightened. He said, Marie,
Marie, hold on tight. And down we went.

These lines were taken verbatim, as Joyce would have done, from a conversation Eliot had had with Countess Marie Larisch. The image is in flux: it approximates the quality of a remembered impression—the commingling of memory and emotion that will prove to be unforgettable.

When Lil's husband got demobbed, I said
I didn't mince my words, I said to her myself,
HURRY UP PLEASE IT'S TIME
Now Albert's coming back, make yourself a bit smart.
He'll want to know what you done with that money he gave you
To get yourself some teeth. He did, I was there.
You have them all out, Lil, and get a nice set,
He said, I swear, I can't bear to look at you.
And no more can't I, I said, and think of poor Albert,
He's been in the army four years, he wants a good time,
And if you don't give it him, there's others will, I said.
Oh is there, she said. Something o' that, I said.
Then I'll know who to thank, she said, and give me a straight look.

Numberless realistic novels, yet to be written, were compressed in this passage. A few years before, Joyce had written:

"Good-night, Gabriel. Good-night, Gretta!"
"Good-night, Aunt Kate, and thanks ever so much. Good-night, Aunt Julia."
"O, good-night, Gretta, I didn't see you."
"Good-night, Mr. D'Arcy. Good-night, Miss O'Callaghan."
"Good-night, Miss Morkan."
"Good-night, again."
"Good-night, all. Safe home."
"Good-night. Good-night."

To which Eliot appended:

Goonight Bill. Goonight Lou. Goonight May. Goonight.
Ta ta. Goonight. Goonight.
Good night, ladies, good night, sweet ladies, good night, good night.

In a poem of less than 450 lines, Eliot sounds the chords that will provide a generation with innumerable themes and variations. The technical innovations are an integral part of the imagery.

She turns and looks a moment in the glass,
Hardly aware of her departed lover;
Her brain allows one half-formed thought to pass:
'Well now that's done: and I'm glad it's over.'
When lovely woman stoops to folly and
Paces about her room again, alone,
She smoothes her hair with automatic hand,
And puts a record on the gramophone.

These images are like lighted windows in a dark structure. They do not accumulate to form a single picture, but remain tableaux, haunting in their separateness, like the tarot cards of Madame Sosostris, "known to be the wisest woman in Europe."

. . . Here, said she,
Is your card, the drowned Phoenician Sailor,
(Those are pearls that were his eyes. Look!)
Here is Belladonna, the Lady of the Rocks,
The lady of situations.

The reader's freedom to interpret these cards, as he will, or as he must, enhances their effect on the imagination. The didactic grain of Eliot's nature, stridently evident in his criticism, is remarkably absent from the poetry. Dry places, rattling bones, clutching roots, stony rubbish, trees that give no shelter, wells that give no water are abundant and tiresome, but they present themselves as images, not arguments.

In calling this poem *The Waste Land*, the poet provided a concept that was itself an image congenial to the American imagination. Postwar disillusion was eager for its appropriate icon. Eliot's images anticipated the blight Sandburg was celebrating in *Smoke and Steel*.

At the violet hour, when the eyes and back
Turn upward from the desk, when the human engine waits

Like a taxi throbbing waiting,
I Tiresias, though blind, throbbing between two lives,
Old man with wrinkled female breasts, can see
At the violet hour, the evening hour that strives
Homeward, and brings the sailor home from sea,
The typist home at teatime, clears her breakfast, lights
Her stove, and lays out food in tins.
Out of the window perilously spread
Her drying combinations touched by the sun's last rays,
On the divan are piled (at night her bed)
Stockings, slippers, camisoles, and stays.
I Tiresias, old man with wrinkled dugs
Perceived the scene, and foretold the rest—

The poet would soon find this too easy, too resembling of what it anticipated, the trick of it too easily mimicked, unprotected by the neglect customary to difficult poetry.

A metaphysical poet, Eliot is obsessed with the reality behind the appearance. How was this to be imaged?

Who is the third who walks always beside you?
When I count, there are only you and I together
But when I look ahead up the white road
There is always another one walking beside you
Gliding wrapt in a brown mantle, hooded
I do not know whether a man or a woman
—But who is that on the other side of you?

This defies an exact interpretation. The reader is compelled to an imaginative response that is in itself a form of image-making.

In "Burnt Norton" he writes:

Garlic and sapphires in the mud
Clot the bedded axle-tree.
The trilling wire in the blood
Sings below inveterate scars
And reconciles forgotten wars.

In "East Coker":

Dawn points, and another day

Prepares for heat and silence. Out at sea the dawn wind
Wrinkles and slides. . . .

And in summary:

So here I am, in the middle way, having had twenty years—
Twenty years largely wasted, the years of *l'entre deux guerres*—
Trying to learn to use words, and every attempt
Is a wholly new start, and a different kind of failure
Because one has only learnt to get the better of words
For the thing one no longer has to say, or the way in which
One is no longer disposed to say it. And so each venture
Is a new beginning, a raid on the inarticulate
With shabby equipment always deteriorating
In the general mess of imprecision of feeling,
Undisciplined squads of emotion. . . .

The dialect of the tribe, thus honed and purified, returns the
traveler to the point of departure, in the hope that he will
know it for the first time.

I do not know much about gods; but I think that the river
Is a strong brown god—sullen, untamed and intractable,
Patient to some degree, at first recognized as a frontier;
Useful, untrustworthy, as a conveyor of commerce;
Then only a problem confronting the builder of bridges.

This is not the Sweet Thames, scene of departed nymphs,
but the "big muddy" below St. Louis:

Time the destroyer is time the preserver,
Like the river with its cargo of dead Negroes, cows and chicken
    coops,
The bitter apple and the bite in the apple.

Home is where one starts from. As we grow older
The world becomes stranger, the pattern more complicated
Of dead and living. . . .

It will be of little interest to future readers of this poet if
*The Waste Land* is largely a personal matter, an interior
landscape, or the cunningly manipulated parallel of a genera-

tion's disenchantment. What matters will prove to be the image-making that captivates the imagination.

We have lingered in the chambers of the sea
By sea-girls wreathed with seaweed red and brown
Till human voices wake us, and we drown.

# Katherine Anne Porter

To be fully conscious, to be one of those on whom nothing is lost, is to be aware of the ceaseless overlapping of the past and the present. This past might embrace history, as in Joyce, or be intimately personal, as in Proust, or pervasive and diffuse, as in James. In Katherine Anne Porter its haunting presence determines the subtlety and range of her style, and its civilized tone. The emerging and soon prevailing vernacular, unique when dealing with the surface of life, as in Lardner, veered away from the conscious-unconscious past it was her nature to acknowledge. However vibrant and intense, however lyrically persuasive, however appealing the sound, look and feel of the present, if the dead were not part of the quick she knew the larger part of conscious life was lacking.

"Flowering Judas," one of her first stories, is compact of conflicting centers of awareness in the consciousness of Laura, the heroine. The setting is Mexico, plainly defined on the map, but in its nature a bizarre and imaginary province, having much in common with Bosch's "The Garden of Earthly Delights." Truly exotic realms either demoralize the artist or awaken and challenge faculties long dormant. Laura's story is memorable because the writer incorporated the malaise and disquiet of her situation, rather than rejecting or attempting to overcome it. A more prudent and experienced writer might have postponed such a test for later consideration. There is always, in Mexico, a growing apprehension of physical and moral disquiet, a sense of derangement—enhanced by the *turista*—that defies treatment and localization. Laura feels "a slow chill, a purely physical sense of danger, a warning in her blood that violence, mutilation, a shocking death, wait for her with lessening impatience."

> Braggioni catches her glance solidly as if he had been waiting for it, leans forward, balancing his paunch between his spread knees, and sings with tremendous emphasis, weighing his words. He has, the song relates, no father and no mother, nor even a friend to console him; lonely as a wave of the sea he comes and goes, lonely as a wave. His mouth opens round and yearns sideways, his balloon cheeks grow oily with the labor of the song. He bulges marvellously in his expensive garments. Over his lavender collar, crushed upon a purple necktie, held by a diamond hoop; over his ammunition belt of tooled leather worked in silver, buckled cruelly around his gasping middle: over the tops of his glossy yellow shoes Braggioni swells with ominous ripeness, his mauve silk hose stretched taut, his ankles bound with the stout leather thongs of his shoes.

This matchless image of the bulging Braggioni displays and summarizes the vital elements of the story, and all that lures, threatens and confuses Laura. Braggioni symbolizes the self-serving sensuality that is so easily confused with passion. His perfumed bulk, his overlapping layers of coveted flesh, all of it adorned like an object of worship, is inexhaustibly suggestive. The very grossness of Braggioni enhances his appeal. His self-indulgent image persists on the mind's eye as Laura goes about her own passionless business. "We are more alike than you realize in some things," he tells her, and it is her knowledge of this fact that haunts, confuses and condemns her. In his boorishness, his childishness, his ceaseless self-gratification, he is also more vitally alive and redeemable than Laura judges herself. The symbol of the flowering judas is a literary touch (out of Eliot's "Gerontion") highly prized in the symbol-ravished twenties, but contributing little to a writer whose symbols are at ease among her images.

> Maria and Miranda, aged twelve and eight years, knew they were young, though they felt they had lived a long time. They had lived not only their own years; but their memories, it seemed to them, began years before they were born, in the lives of the grownups around them, old people above forty, most of them, who had a way of insisting that they too had been young once. It was hard to believe.

This passage from *Old Mortality* is a characteristic image from the author's album. The intermingling of past and present, common to those over forty, is made poignant through the eyes of the girls.

> No, Maria and Miranda found it impossible to sympathize with those young persons, sitting rather stiffly before the camera, hopelessly out of fashion; but they were drawn and held by the mysterious love of the living, who remembered and cherished these dead. The visible remains were nothing; they were dust, perishable as the flesh; the features stamped on paper and metal were nothing, but their living memory enchanted the little girls.

These words call to mind Joyce's story "The Dead," where the living and the dead are inextricably mingled. Both writers rely on irony to check the flow of writer (and reader) emotion. Both writers, however astringent, are unabashed romantics. *These* are the things that matter. Never mind how absurd they may appear. This assurance of knowing what matters, and the bottomless depths of personal involvement, gives the history of the little girls a memorable dimension. Part of it lies in our assurance that the story is close to history. The narrative takes its shape, and shows the strain, of being faithful to more than fiction. If it has the grace and charm of a fine writer at ease with her appropriate material, it also has the occasional tautness of a transcription. It often seems more memoir than fiction, using the standards of judgment the author herself has established, involving the reader, as the writer is involved,

with the troubled consciousness of Miranda, to the point of her
open rebellion. The resolution she achieves, in which both the
present and the past are acknowledged, is withheld from the
reader to the last word in the story. Caught up in her fury, her
frustration, the liberation that she feels to be free of her
entrapment, it is the reader who shares the poignant awaken-
ing that is held in reserve for Miranda.

> . . . Ah, but there is my own life to come yet, she thought, my
> own life now and beyond. I don't want any promises, I won't have
> false hopes, I won't be romantic about myself. I can't live in their
> world any longer, she told herself, listening to the voices back of
> her. Let them tell their stories to each other. Let them go on
> explaining how things happened. I don't care. At least I can know
> the truth about what happens to me, she assured herself silently,
> making a promise to herself, in her hopefulness, her ignorance.

Miranda's soliloquy summarizes the story in terms of her
widening (she believes) perspective. It skillfully gains and
holds the reader's attention through its repeated use of phrases
that are usually intrusive: she "speaks to herself," she "asks
herself," she "tells herself and assures herself," in such a
manner that the irony of her assurance is self-evident but the
reader is not consciously aware of it. He is carried away, as she
is, to the unexpected truth of her resolution.

Until the reader is alerted to the exactness of her prose, the
fine texture of her humor, the intricate play of hard facts and
mocking ironies, he might not think *Noon Wine* is by the same
author. The time is about the turn of the century, the scene a
small farm in Texas. A hired hand, Mr. Helton, has just asked
the owner of the farm for work.

> When Mr. Thompson expected to drive a bargain he always
> grew very hearty and jovial. There was nothing wrong with him
> except that he hated like the devil to pay wages. He said so
> himself. . . .
> "Now, what I want to know is, how much you fixing to gouge
> outa me?" he brayed, slapping his knee. After he had kept it up as
> long as he could, he quieted down, feeling a little sheepish, and

cut himself a chew. Mr. Helton was staring out somewhere between the barn and the orchard, and seemed to be sleeping with his eyes open.

The precision and fluency of the writing are characteristic of Miss Porter. The vernacular texture of life, its voice and tone are flawlessly recorded. Comparatively "simple folk" are perceived to be as subtly responsive, as obsessively motivated, as profoundly vulnerable, as the more intellectual ornaments of fiction. The writer knows that the craft of such a story is writing up to such people, not down to them. To my mind she knows them better than Faulkner, who habitually and compulsively projects on his creations his own hallucinations. Evil, evil incarnate, appears in the form of Homer T. Hatch. Here is Mr. Thompson's first glimpse of him:

> He wasn't exactly a fat man. He was more like a man who had been fat recently. His skin was baggy and his clothes were too big for him, and he somehow looked like a man who should be fat, ordinarily, but who might have just got over a spell of sickness. Mr. Thompson didn't take to his looks at all, he couldn't say why.

The achievement of this description is that we feel with assurance that Mr. Thompson is right, although we can't say why. In some inscrutable manner, free of the author's conniving, we feel privy to an insight that is not to be questioned.

> The fat man opened his mouth and roared with joy, showing rabbit teeth brown as shoe-leather. Mr. Thompson saw nothing to laugh at, for once. . . .

By such stages the reader experiences Mr. Thompson's growing disquiet. He feels an apprehension that eludes description. The fat man has long made it his business to round up dangerous "escaped loonatics." The hired hand Mr. Helton, he claims, is one of them. Twelve years before, in an argument with his brother, who had borrowed one of Mr. Helton's harmonicas and lost it, he had run him through with a pitchfork.

> ". . . Now fact is [Mr. Hatch tells Mr. Thompson], in the last

twelve years or so I musta rounded up twenty-odd escaped loonatics, besides a couple of escaped convicts that I just run into by accident, like. . . . Fact is, I'm for law and order, I don't like to see lawbreakers and loonatics at large. It ain't the place for them. Now I reckon you're bound to agree with me on that, aren't you?"

Mr. Thompson is confused and demoralized.

. . . [he] couldn't think how to describe how it was with Mr. Helton. "Why, he's been like one of the family," he said, "the best stand-by a man ever had." Mr. Thompson tried to see his way out. It was a fact Mr. Helton might go loony again any minute, and now this fellow talking around the country would put Mr. Thompson in a fix. It was a terrible position. He couldn't think of any way out. "You're crazy," Mr. Thompson roared suddenly, "you're the crazy one around here, you're crazier than he ever was! You get off this place or I'll handcuff you and turn you over to the law. You're trespassing," shouted Mr. Thompson. "Get out of here before I knock you down!"

At this moment of disorder Mr. Helton intervenes; he is knifed by Mr. Hatch, who is axed down by Mr. Thompson. The steps that led, inexorably, to this explosion of violence, now lead as inevitably away from it. Mr. Thompson is doomed. Piece by piece, shred by shred, the ties that bound him to people loosen. His wife and sons turn against him. In a manner not dissimilar to Mr. Helton, he is left alone with his torment; his only options are madness or self-destruction. The reader knows as plainly as if he had lived it that the flowering evil lies in the subsoil of man's nature, and is the property of Homer T. Hatch, vile as he is. If Henry James had grasped that people were somehow more substantial than his impressions of them, he might have written a similar tale of unforced, inevitable human baseness, but the nature of his gift turned him back upon his inexhaustible self.

In the happiest circumstances, the writer of fiction aspires to be the medium rather than the creator, a necessary but not intrusive presence through whom we sense the *other*, and share experience. Miss Porter's fine-grained craft is always present, but in *Pale Horse, Pale Rider* it is also transparent. We neither see nor feel it, and it seems gratuitous to discuss it. Within the compass of a short novel it is exhaustive on a large subject. The writer who deals with consciousness as revealed through events, rather than the larger spectacle of human affairs, will find that short fiction tends to grow longer, and the longer fiction somewhat shorter than the common practice. This is true of Miss Porter as it was of Virginia Woolf, a writer so attentive to consciousness it emerged as her subject. However appealing in theory, consciousness as a subject is restrictive and self-defeating in practice, luring the writer to shape the world in his own image. Self-images would displace the essential facts of Mr. Thompson, Mr. Helton and Homer T. Hatch. However defensible, theoretically, and however brilliant the execution, this practice is death to fiction and terminates in silence. This, happily, has not proved to be Miss Porter's problem. She keeps a firm grip on the soiled hand, as well as the pure, the frivolous and the sleazy. Although the downward path to wisdom is an insight that informs most of her fiction, its effect on the reader is one of life enhancement, rather than life negation. We are impressed by its truth, and this truth is liberating.

> Granite walls, whirlpools, stars are things. None of them is death, nor the image of it. Death is death, said Miranda, and for the dead it has no attributes. Silenced she sank easily through deeps under deeps of darkness until she lay like a stone at the farthest bottom of life, knowing herself to be blind, deaf, speechless, no longer aware of the members of her own body, entirely withdrawn from all human concerns, yet alive with a peculiar lucidity and coherence; all notions of the mind, the reasonable inquiries of doubt, all ties of blood and the desires of the heart, dissolved and fell away from her, and there remained of her only a minute fiercely burning particle of being that knew itself alone, that relied upon nothing beyond itself for its strength; not susceptible to any appeal or inducement, being itself composed entirely of one single motive, the stubborn will to live. . . . Trust me, the hard unwinking angry point of light said. Trust me. I stay.

# The Ghostly Rumble
# Among the Drums

One of the many paradoxes of the postwar decade was the intermingling of euphoria and disenchantment. An immense release of sentiment and energy, part of the postwar liberation, transformed and exalted individual experience. The Chicago of Dreiser, an impersonal, devouring monster, became the alluring windy city of Sandburg, hog butcher to the world, the night sky lit up with the lyricism of smoke and steel. Fifty years before they symbolize death and pollutants, they lift and charge the spirit as signs of progress. In the not quite technical glory of full and vibrant color, the steel furnaces of Gary, the spectacle of urban traffic, the accumulating grit and filth of industrial grime make their appearance on calendars and catalogues distributed to farms without electric lights or indoor plumbing. After they'd seen Paree, how keep the boys down on the farm?

For this blowoff of animal spirits and psychic energy the vernacular provides the safety valve. Everybody speaks it, hears it, understands it. With each passing day more and more write and read it. Everybody, unconsciously, contributes to an aggregate act of the imagination, a disorderly but fertile flow of creation. In no previous culture had so many participated in the coinage of a new language. The European novel, approaching a summit in the works of Mann, Joyce and Proust, gives way, in American practice, to the fiction of self-fulfillment. In writing a novel the writer searched for himself, found himself, developed himself. Thanks to the vernacular no literary barrier distinguished between one life and another. Hobos wrote about hobos, doughboys about doughboys, poor boys about poor boys, farm boys about farm boys. If every man's life constituted a book, more and more of them felt obligated to write one. Underlying this upsurge of self-expression, of self-appreciation, was an alluring substratum of disenchantment. The more sophisticated writers, having been to war, wrote about it with unexampled candor. To the sophisticated, the bitter apéritif taste of disillusion was much preferred to the cloying sweetness of illusion. Fresh out of illusion, the youth of the twenties experienced the delights of the word "blasé," which a popular song had given currency.

You're deep just like a chasm
You've no enthusiasm
You're tired and uninspired
You're blasé

Your day is one of leisure
In which you search for pleasure
You're bored when you're adored
You're blasé

Although it is commonly felt that literature shaped the consciousness of the postwar "lost" generation, the emotions of the twenties were expressed and sustained by an unprecedented flood of "popular" music. An American will find it hard to believe that this, too, was something new in the world. The great flood of utterance, predicted by Whitman, found its release in song, with appropriate lyrics. These tunes and lyrics saturated the air that bathed the U.S.A. Before he read a word, the reader was well prepared for *This Side of Paradise, The Sun Also Rises*, the numberless novels of bittersweet longing and romance. Sound transformed the movies to sing-alongs with the organ, and the movie house became the scene of a brief release and celebration. Gershwin's *Rhapsody in Blue* captured the soaring, yearning, swooning sense of soulful elevation: the overflow of this sentiment spread the delta that made the Beatles and the rock of the sixties possible. The blithe euphoria of Dixie, the sweet sorrows of the blues, the driving force and fire of Louis Armstrong's "Shine," were alternating currents tingling the flesh and nerve ends; the dissolution of the words in Armstrong's scatting acknowledged the transcendent role of the rhythm. Wordless, this music admitted to no barrier, cut across all lines and was free as the air. In the big cities the stages enthroned the big bands, prodigally dispensing glory and dreams. Great songs, great bands, great singers crackled on the air waves, and in the heat of the summer filled the night with the intoxication of longing that fevered the blood and mind of Jay Gatsby, who had vowed to waste no more time at Shafter's. The single magical catalyst of this diffuse charge of emotion was the mute Lone Eagle, Charles A. Lindbergh, who single-handedly (in the style of the sports heroes Jack Dempsey, Babe Ruth, Red Grange, Bill Tilden) took off into the glory of the wild blue yonder—a territory staked out by the words and music. The words might be silly, insipid or corny—or they might be memorable and poignant—but the tune was what mattered, with its ghostly rumble among the drums, and an asthmatic whisper among the trombones. The optimism of Dixie, the nostalgia of the blues charged the air with a shared intoxication. In his bizarre clowning, and his disciplined writing, Scott Fitzgerald perfectly articulated the squads of undisciplined emotion fermenting in the music. If we listen we can hear its subdued accompaniment to his fiction. In the lyrical passages, he could not suppress the words that Cole Porter would put to music.

> . . . I remember the fur coats of the girls returning from Miss-This-or-That's and the chatter of frozen breath and the hands waving overhead as we caught sight of old acquaintances, and the matchings of invitations. . . .

It is the function of such a writer to be carried away. Hemingway would have found this self-exposure embarrassing. Thomas Wolfe was open to the romance of trains, and composed a long tone poem on this subject, but Hemingway, a romantic by nature, suppressed the sentiment as he would an impairment. In Fitzgerald sentiment blows about like pollen, and frequently betrays the appropriate emotion, but Hemingway spared himself such exposure by adopting the attitude of detachment, of toughness. In the writing it often made very good reading.

> ... Wilson, who was ahead was kneeling shooting, and Macomber, as he fired, unhearing his shot in the roaring of Wilson's gun, saw fragments like slate burst from the huge boss of the horns, and the head jerked, he shot again at the wide nostrils and saw the horns jolt again and fragments fly. ...

In the living, however, the suppression of sentiment can be detected in the posture of the writer. He fears the charging beast less than he does the open fly of sentiment. It is sentiment, an excess of it, that produced the remarkable decades between the wars, and the extremes of sentiment, expressed and suppressed, are realized in Hemingway and Fitzgerald. Between these extremes a galaxy of writers published thousands of stories and novels, a few of them great, many of them very good, most of them worth the effort and torment of the writing, all of them testifying to the liberating power of the vernacular as an image-maker.

# Scott Fitzgerald

... The truth was that for some months he had been going through that partitioning of the things of youth wherein it is decided whether or not to die for what one no longer believes. In the dead white hours in Zurich staring into a stranger's pantry across the upshine of a streetlamp, he used to think that he wanted to be good, he wanted to be kind, he wanted to be brave and wise, but it was all pretty difficult. He wanted to be loved, too, if he could fit it in.

This is Scott Fitzgerald designing his own badge of courage, joining his own refined and sentimental torment to that of Miss Porter's Miranda, the strain and illusion of emerging self-awareness, making a promise to himself in his hopefulness, his ignorance.

The style of Fitzgerald, its appealing soft focus, blending youthful sentiment and mature observation, derived more from British than American examples. He had read and admired Compton Mackenzie. Fitzgerald is the least innovative, the least vernacular of the writers who were his friends and peers. "Do read something other," Edmund Wilson wrote him, "than contemporary British novelists." That an American writer of the twenties should need this advice is remarkable. The chronicler of the jazz age, one of the truly lost of the lost generation, felt no urgent need to depart from the cultivated

voice of a young man educated at Princeton. Writing to his
editor, Max Perkins, about the jacket for his first novel:

> Who picks out the cover? I'd like something that could be a
> set—look cheerful and important like a Shaw book. I notice Shaw,
> Galsworthy and Barrie do that. But Wells doesn't—I wonder
> why?

No American writer in that listing. Nor would it have
crossed Fitzgerald's mind to apprentice himself as a journalist.
He *knew* how to write. That was why he had gone to college.
Hemingway's example would have struck him as incredulous.
Neither did it cross his mind to go in search of experience. He
had *had* experience. It was all within him. Experience was
simply how he felt. For romantic experience he needed a girl,
and he had a girl.

These details are of interest because this writer, in his short
productive life, did not depart from them. Experience was
emotion: emotion revealed itself in sentiment. He made no
experiments, he suffered no creative torments in shaping the
language to his purpose. Why should he? He needed only to
say how he felt. He missed the *real* war (experienced by Dos
Passos, Hemingway and Faulkner), but experience of the war
would not have schooled him to the facts of his nature. He
would have died a hero's death, or he would have returned to
a hero's welcome. Emotion would have transformed events
into heart's desire.

How did this non-innovative writer cast a spell over blasé,
sophisticated, thrill-hungry readers? Sentiment distilled to an
essence. Sentiment is present in all the writing of the decade
but in Fitzgerald it is there in saturation.

> . . . Now it was a cool night with that mysterious excitement in
> it which comes at the two changes of the year. The quiet lights in
> the houses were humming out into the darkness and there was a
> stir and bustle among the stars. Out of the corner of his eye
> Gatsby saw that the blocks of the sidewalks really formed a ladder
> and mounted to a secret place above the trees—he could climb to
> it, if he climbed alone, and once there he could suck on the pap of
> life, gulp down the incomparable milk of wonder.

This incomparable milk of wonder is not for strong stomachs. That Fitzgerald and his readers found it intoxicating is part of the thralldom of the new, popular music, the appropriate medium for such sentiments. More than anything else in this fabled, fertile decade, jazz determined the texture of emotional life.

Daisy began to sing with the music in a husky, rhythmic whisper, bringing out a meaning in each word that it had never had before and would never have again. When the melody rose her voice broke up sweetly, following it, in a way contralto voices have, and each change tipped out a little of her warm human magic up on the air.

Years later, in *Tender Is the Night:*

. . . Afterward he played some Schubert songs and some new jazz from America that Nicole hummed in her harsh, sweet contralto over his shoulder.

"Thank y' fathe-r
"Thank y' moth-r
"Thanks for meetingup with one another—"
"I don't like that one," Dick said, starting to turn the page.
"Oh, play it!" she exclaimed. "Am I going through the rest of life flinching at the word 'father'?"
"—Thank the horse that pulled the buggy that night!
Thank you both for being justabit tight—"

In *Echoes of the Jazz Age:*

. . . Sometimes, though, there is a ghostly rumble among the drums, an asthmatic whisper in the trombones that swings me back into the early twenties when we drank wood alcohol and every day in every way grew better and better, and there was a first abortive shortening of skirts, and girls all looked alike in sweater dresses, and people you didn't want to know said "yes, we have no bananas," and it seemed only a question of a few years before the older people would step aside and let the world be run by those who saw things as they were—

He wanted to be good, he wanted to be kind, and he wanted to be loved—if he could just fit it in. This flawlessly narcissistic sentiment strained the tolerance of some readers, but found its perfect expression in the whisper of the trombones, the rumble of the drums.

> ... My own happiness in the past often approached such an ecstasy that I could not share it even with the person dearest to me but had to walk it away in quiet streets and lanes with only fragments of it to distill into little lines in books. . . .

Hemingway mocks the sentiment and the admission: Fitzgerald admits to the crippling effects:

> Through all he said [Gatsby], even through his appalling sentimentality, I was reminded of something—an elusive rhythm, a fragment of lost words, that I had heard somewhere a long time ago. For a moment a phrase tried to take shape in my mouth and my lips parted like a dumb man's, as though there was more struggling upon them than a wisp of startled air. But they made no sound, and what I had almost remembered was uncommunicable forever.

Sentiment is not quickly or easily responsive to innovation. *Dis*enchantment is the appropriate mode of sophistication. Only Fitzgerald could, without self-mockery, have entitled a novel *Tender Is the Night* more than a decade after *This Side of Paradise*. In an effort to sustain the necessary thralldom, the style departs from the brash jazz-age assertiveness to echo the colors and images of popular fancy, the literature of romance that catered to women.

> The hotel and its bright tan prayer rug of beach were one. In the early morning the distant image of Cannes, the pink and cream of the old fortifications, the purple Alp that bounded Italy, were cast across the water and lay quavering in ripples and rings sent up by sea-plants through the clear shallows.

That these lines were described as a beautiful barbarism attest to the widely shared nostalgia of exile. Hemingway had recently published *Death in the Afternoon*. The pink and cream fortifications, the prayer rug of the beach, the purple Alp that bounded Italy were as real to Fitzgerald as the retreat from Caporetto. Unqualified happiness insists on this unqualified sentiment. In this unlikely context he proposes to sound the emotional disarray of his generation. To a qualified extent he succeeded.

> Nicole kept in touch with Dick after her new marriage; there were letters on business matters, and about the children. When she said, as she often did, "I loved Dick and I'll never forget him," Tommy answered, "Of course not—why should you?"

This answer with a question that remains unanswered, which we know to be unanswerable, is characteristic of Fitzgerald's need to hold contrarieties in balance. The sentiment may fail him, but he will not fail the sentiment. For all of his appalling sentimentality—or we might say because of it—he knew more about the native's unquiet desperation than those who spoke out with more assurance. For all of his self-indulgence, this unlikely man had the courage to admit to what he knew, and what he didn't know.

It is of interest that the two lyricists of sentiment, Fitzgerald and Wolfe, would prove to be traditional as stylists, glancing backward, rather than forward, for notes that chimed with their emotions. Wolfe, however, found it hard to distinguish between what he had read and what he was feeling.

> He turned, and saw her then, and so finding her, was lost, and so losing self, was found, and s⁻ seeing her, saw for a fading moment only the pleasant image of the woman that perhaps she was, and that life saw. He never knew: he knew only that from that moment his spirit was impaled upon the knife of love. From that moment on he never was again to lose her utterly, never to wholly repossess unto himself the lonely, wild integrity of youth which had been his. . . .

Wolfe is impaled upon clichés, not the knife of love, and finds himself at a loss how to choose among them. The choking overcharge of emotion is felt by the author, but not by the reader. Fitzgerald is the superior of the two image-makers since he often found the metaphor for his emotion. How ill he served, but how well he knew himself.

> "That's my Middle West [he wrote in *Gatsby*] not the wheat or

the prairies or the lost Swede towns, but the thrilling returning trains of my youth, and the street lamps and the sleigh bells in the frosty dark and the shadows of holly wreaths thrown by lighted windows on the snow."

Fitzgerald was experienced with the follies of American sentiment—the careless people who smashed up things and people, then retreated back into their money, and their carelessness—but he mistook the frustrations of their, and his own, egotism as the substance of tragic emotion. It is this that makes *The Crack-Up* more embarrassing than contemptible, as some readers found it. His air of mourning is less for lost life than life's betrayal of his own fiction. Commensurate with his capacity for hope and wonder was his instinct for candor, the self-revelation that some of his peers found questionable. Having overdrawn his other resources, he scraped the bottom of his own barrel.

> So what? This is what I think now: that the natural state of the sentient adult is a qualified unhappiness.

This fall from happiness, unqualified, is the death of the world of sentiment. The child suckled on the fresh green breast of the world and the man who had held his breath in the presence of this enthrallment shared at world's end a common disenchantment.

> . . . I thought of Gatsby's wonder when he first picked out the green light at the end of Daisy's dock. He had come a long way to this blue lawn, and his dream must have seemed so close that he could hardly fail to grasp it. He did not know that it was already behind him, somewhere back in that vast obscurity beyond the city, where the dark fields of the republic rolled on under the night.

Keenly aware of the slings and arrows of personal misfortune, including self-abuses, the poet of sentiment is mercifully blind to the pathos of his situation. A high cold star on a winter's night is the refrain of a tune with the words missing, like the vapor of breath from the mouth of a girl with her lips parted. A song without words.

# John Dos Passos

In his praise of Joyce, T. S. Eliot spoke of his method as "... simply a way of controlling, of ordering, of giving shape and significance to the immense panorama of futility and anarchy which is contemporary history...." Contemporary history continues to be a problem for the writer of fiction. Not many writers now feel, as they once felt, that their example of order will do more than give and shape significance to a novel (to which history was vastly indifferent), but many postwar writers found it necessary to believe that their novels could and must change the world. How could free men accept a panorama of futility and anarchy? One such writer was John Dos Passos, a young man well favored by circumstance but profoundly disturbed by social injustice. Of the gifted young men of his generation Dos Passos was the most exemplary, neither starry-eyed nor self-indulgent, like Fitzgerald, nor macho-tough and egocentric, like Hemingway, but a generous, affectionate young man for whom ideals were principles. He accepted his personal good luck as a trust he would share with others. Numberless young men of his quality, green from the playing fields of Eton, had been tested and slaughtered in France, leaving to the war-baptized American survivors the burden of their story. The scale and disorder of that event led most writers to avert their eyes and live with their horror. Dos

Passos wrote *Three Soldiers,* published a few months later than Fitzgerald's *This Side of Paradise.* The jazz age could hardly have opened with more contrasting prospects. Fitzgerald missed the war, but we might well wonder what war he would have survived. There is no place in his nature for such an obliteration of self. Five years later he writes *The Great Gatsby,* and almost ten years later *Tender Is the Night,* marvelous evocations of life still this side of paradise. Little of the world's futility and anarchy penetrates this universe of heart's desire.

By his nature and experience, Dos Passos is compelled to incorporate more of the world as it is into his fiction. He makes an innovative start with *Manhattan Transfer,* a collective portrait of New York. Here, as in the novels that follow, the individual personality is subordinate to social circumstance, numbers and forces. The trilogy comprising *U.S.A.—The 42nd Parallel, 1919* and *The Big Money*—is the most ambitious effort of an American writer to impose shape and significance on the immense panorama of American life in the first three decades of this century. The very conception of such a project waited on the ripening of the vernacular. It is the language that speaks, describes and proves to be responsive to social forces.

> It was a bright metalcolored January day when Charley went downtown to lunch with Nat Benton. He got to the broker's office a little early, and sat waiting in an empty office looking out through the broad steelframed windows at the North River and the Statue of Liberty and the bay beyond all shiny ruffled green in the northwest wind, spotted with white dabs of smoke from tugboats, streaked with catspaws and the churny wakes of freighters bucking the wind, checkered with lighters and flatboats, carferries, barges and the red sawedoff passengerferries. A schooner with grey sails was running out before the wind.

This image wavers between that of Charley's stream of semiconsciousness and the impersonal voice of the narrator. If we compare it with a passage from Katherine Anne Porter, we note that the *consciousness* is minimal. The roving camera eye remains on the surface, the tone and texture of the writing is simplistic. One of Ring Lardner's hicks, on a visit to the city, might have sat daydreaming in such a manner. The repetitions are grating rather than pleasing. Dos Passos is careful to minimize the romantic allurements of the "big city." The image glitters, it is full of "things" but it has no depth and resists penetration. Insofar as the reader is able to determine, it is the world that Charley lives in. He is as much a piece of it as the steelframed windows, the Statue of Liberty, the carferries, the barges, the sawedoff passengerferries. The style has the breezy glare of Coney Island with flapping banners and windblown snatches of music. If it is the writer's purpose to play down the character, and play up the context, in this passage he has succeeded. Charley is there, in the way all the rest of it is *there*.

The first pages of *The 42nd Parallel* or *The Big Money*, two volumes of the *U.S.A.* trilogy, give the reader a sensation that is rare in American fiction—a sense of being outside, rather than inside, the protagonists. What the author wants is the panorama, the reader poised or in movement above it, low enough to sense the movement and appreciate the details. Only such a perspective will correct the misconceptions the characters have of themselves and each other. They believe what they have been told. They do not see what they have become. Zola and Dreiser have shared this perspective, but from a lower, less comprehensive elevation. The reader who read each book as it appeared, over a period of six years, experienced a somewhat mind-expanding sense of scale that lacked human details. The characters were difficult to latch on to. The mind-expanding overview was at the expense of individual attachments. The destructive forces of the society— to a reader of novels—also became mechanical and monotonous. Dos Passos erred in believing—as believers are inclined to err—that the reader must grovel if he is to fathom groveling. The ceaseless flow of the vernacular is like the background of noise in a bus station.

A couple of days later the old women put on their best black silk shawls and took the baby to the church to be christened. Its little face looked awful blue in the middle of all the lace they dressed it in. That night it turned almost black. In the morning it was dead. Tony cried and the old women carried on and they spent a lot of money on a little white casket with silver handles and a hearse and a priest for the funeral.

This is a parody of the writer's intent: the chords are struck but give off no sound. The scale of his effort betrayed the fiction, and resulted in wads of verbal padding. In this panorama of aggregate disorder the insights do not keep pace with the flood of information. There is abundant observation, at the expense of insightful, fictive perception. The author feels this is dictated by the overview, and his position *au-dessus le mêlée,* from which he fortunately departs in the "Newsreel" and the "camera-eye" passages between chapters. These original and innovative portraits give the full measure of Dos Passos's talent.

> Veblen,
> a greyfaced shambling man lolling resentful at his desk with his cheek on his hand, in a low sarcastic mumble of intricate phrases subtly paying out the logical inescapable rope of matteroffact for a society to hang itself by . . .

This image-making is fresh; it is still audacious, and antici-pates fiction now being written and at the time quickly copied. But the great burden of the demonstration, like the scene itself, proved unrewarding. The literate reader gets the mes-sage early, and finds the long demonstration tiresome. Dos Passos had an intricate social purpose—he passionately desired to save the republic—but when the republic failed to collapse, the urgency of his message vanished.

> The young man waits at the edge of the concrete, with one hand he grips a rubbed suitcase of phony leather, the other hand almost making a fist, thumb up
> that moves in ever so slight an arc when a car slithers past, a truck roars clatters; the wind of cars passing ruffles his hair, slaps grit in his face.

Head swims, hunger has twisted the belly tight,
    he has skinned a heel through the torn sock, feet ache in the broken shoes, under the threadbare suit carefully brushed off with the hand, the torn drawers have a crummy feel, the feel of having slept in your clothes; in the nostrils lingers the staleness of discouraged carcasses crowded into a transient camp, the carbolic stench of the jail, on the taut cheeks the shamed flush from the boring eyes of cops and deputies. . . .

This explicitly detailed image has all the signs of pathos but none of its emotion. The old suitcase, the phony leather, the skinned heel, the torn sock, the crummy feel of slept-in clothes are swatches of discarded clichés. They have become "ready-mades," through use and abuse, signals that evoke pat responses. The vibrant surface of life that captivated Whitman and launched a new age of image-making has become so commonplace the image is a token for the emotion. As Eliot had anticipated:

Among the smoke and fog of a December afternoon
You have the scene arrange itself—as it will seem to do—
With "I have saved this afternoon for you" . . .

A stand-in for the emotion, the cliché now generates fiction that seems to write itself. James M. Cain's *The Postman Always Rings Twice* was written at the same time as *The Big Money*.

Then I saw her. She had been out in back, in the kitchen, but she came in to gather up my dishes. Except for the shape, she really wasn't any raving beauty, but she had a sulky look to her, and her lips stuck out in a way that made me want to mash them in for her.

This image, like a blown-up film clip, provokes the reader to fantasize his own movie. The writer deals in signs, tokens and emblems that are printed on posters, doorways, highways: "CURVES AHEAD," "NO PASSING," "DANGER," with the semaphore message "STOP, LOOK & LISTEN!". At the heart of the Depression, when all the signs are bad, the lights continue to read "GO."

Dos Passos understood this anarchy of the emotions, and he had his moments of triumph.

> Three gulls wheel above the broken boxes, orangerinds, spoiled cabbage heads that heave between the splintered plank walls, the green waves spume under the round bow as the ferry, skidding on the tide, crashes, gulps the broken water, slides, settles slowly into the slip.

This assembly of clichéd materials has been recycled by the writer and suffused with emotion. Too often, however, the scale of his canvas led him to make a collage of ready-made ingredients. Both painters and sculptors had turned this to their advantage, acknowledging the ready-made as a new artifact, but Dos Passos is one of the first to achieve such triumphs in fiction.

> One day at a little restaurant at Golfe Juan she picked up a goodlooking young wop who kept a garage and drove a little Bugatti racer.
> Saying that she might want to buy the car, she made him go to her studio to take her out for a ride;
> her friends didn't want her to go, said he was nothing but a mechanic, she insisted, she'd had a few drinks (there was nothing left she cared for in the world but a few drinks and a goodlooking young man);
> she got in beside him and
> She threw her heavilyfringed scarf round her neck with a big sweep she had and
> turned back and said,
> with the strong California accent her French never lost:
> Adieu, mes amis, je vais à la gloire.

Compare this image of Isadora Duncan with Fitzgerald's portrait of Myrtle Wilson in *The Great Gatsby*. Sentiments, like language, have strained to cracking under the tension, the burden, the slipping and sliding, the ceaseless profusion of verbal images. In Dos Passos we see the dilemma of the writer at the summit of the vernacular triumph, sometimes the master of his talent, sometimes the victim of an assured, grasping, appropriating language. To recover that "easy commerce of the old and the new, the common word exact without vulgarity, the formal word precise but not pedantic," the writer must henceforth purify as well as use the dialect of the tribe.

# William Faulkner

Through the fence, between the curling flower spaces, I could see them hitting. They were coming toward where the flag was and I went along the fence. Luster was hunting in the grass by the flower tree. They took the flag out, and they were hitting. Then they put the flag back and they went to the table, and he hit and the other hit. Then they went on, and I went along the fence. Luster came away from the flower tree and we went along the fence and they stopped and we stopped and I looked through the fence while Luster was hunting in the grass.

Will the reader of modern fiction, or the sportsman who follows golf, have the least difficulty with this passage? Only the reader, perhaps, will get the bloom of it. To see the game of golf through the eyes of the idiot Benjy is a matter of technique rather than psychology. The experiment and preparation of American writers have made this triumph possible. Technique determines the reader's first impression, as it does his first view of a Cubist painting. The reader's puzzlement, and his predictable pleasure in solving the puzzle, is a matter of technically achieved effects. The psychology takes its cues from the technical innovations. It is characteristic of Faulkner's talent to let the seeing eye determine the frame of the picture. The sentences have a visual and audible rhythm, as if the words described the movements of a half-concealed creature closely observed by a hunter.

131

We went along the fence and came to the garden fence, where our shadows were. My shadow was higher than Luster's on the fence. We came to the broken place and went through it.

The repetition of "fence" subtly defines the limited nature of Benjy's vision. Extreme states of consciousness lend themselves, without strain, to vernacular usage, there being little that is natural to man that is alien to this supple language. In addition to the appropriate extremes of emotion, Faulkner wants an effect of extravagance, of unbridled impressions, both expressionistic and romantic. The familiar rhetoric of gothic horror, in its Southern branch, is charged in such a way language crackles:

> . . . a leashed turmoil of lust like so many lowering dogs after a scarce-fledged and apparently unawares bitch.

The master technician Joyce would have appreciated Faulkner's use of the stream of consciousness where consciousness itself was felt to be wanting.

> There was a wisteria vine blooming for the second time that summer on a wooden trellis before one window, into which sparrows came now and then in random gusts, making a dry vivid dusty sound before going away: and opposite Quentin, Miss Coldfield in the eternal black which she had worn for forty-three years now, whether for sister, father, or nothusband none know, sitting so bolt upright in the straight hard chair that was so tall for her that her legs hung straight and rigid as if she had iron shinbones and ankles, clear of the floor with that air of impotent and static rage like children's feet . . .

The reader who attempts to parse this passage into sensible prose misses the picture. It is a word construct that parallels the impressions we receive from Expressionistic painting, one of extreme hallucination. Visible objects vibrate and writhe as in the canvases of van Gogh and Munch. Words are applied to the page like gobs of paint to the canvas with a palette knife. The effect is that of emotions too intense and distorted for words. Munch has a painting entitled "The Cry." The emotion is expressed in swirls of violent, contrasting colors. We recognize that it is on the verge of madness. Munch would have been the ideal artist to have painted Miss Coldfield, in her eternal black, sitting so bolt upright that her legs hung rigid, as if she had iron shinbones and ankles. "Impotent and static rage" has compelled both artists to technical innovations in writing and painting. The discharge of this excess of emotion is usually in terms of violence. There are no Milquetoasts among the Expressionists. Trees and mountains writhe, skies flame, colors shriek and light flares, human faces are red, green, purple and yellow, objects possessed by invisible forces are twisted and contorted. Soutine has painted a strung-up plucked rooster as if it had been *lynched*. No other word is appropriate. In this manner a Russian Jew, living in Paris, combined the impotent rage of the concentration-camp survivor with the American innovation of lynching. These ultimate acts of violence, separated in space, shared a common, barbarous moment in time.

A similar sense of outrage inspired Picasso's "Guernica," where the burden of technique dominated the horror—an act of rage rather than impotence—a re-experiencing of outrage and frustration on the level of innovative image-making. Faulkner is of this breed, although his rage is both literary and highly romantic. Out of the abiding, dreamy and victorious dust he would evoke his indomitable frustration that the past is dead, long live the past. A dry, vivid, dusty sound, a grim, haggard, amazed voice, a hearing sense self-confounded, reveals a writer, for all of his fury, sportively at play in an unexampled language. He is not so provocative as Joyce, but he, too, is an artificer and a shaman, incurably committed to innovation. Faulkner's interest in technique is exhaustive, and often at the expense of his substance. There is too much diffuse emotion, generated by verbal swagger, that strains to pass for good fiction. It is as hard for the reader as it seems to be for the writer to distinguish between the real and the bogus, the words that flow, and flow for no other reason than the spigot is open. Impotent rage, impotent outrage, impotent frustration appear as methodically as slogans, generating neither heat nor light.

> The second convict was short and plump. Almost hairless, he was quite white. He looked like something exposed to light by turning over rotting logs or planks and he too carried (though not in his eyes like the first convict) a sense of burning and impotent outrage.

The colors are here, but repetition has diminished the effect. Again and again these words appear, as if part of the flooding Mississippi's burden of flotsam.

> The bow began to swing back upstream. It turned readily, it outpaced the aghast and outraged instant in which he realized it was swinging far too easily ... his teeth bared in his bloody streaming face while his spent arms flailed the impotent paddle at the water, that innocent-appearing medium which at one time had held him in iron-like and shifting convolutions like an anaconda yet which now seemed to offer no more resistance to the thrust of his urge and need than so much air, like air; the boat ... spinning like a wind vane while he flailed at the water and thought of, envisioned, his companion safe, inactive and at ease in the tree with nothing to do but wait, musing with impotent and terrified fury upon that arbitrariness of human affairs which had abrogated to the one the secure tree and to the other the hysterical and unmanageable boat. . . .

This river is burdened not only with the usual flotsam but the flood tide of words Faulkner uses to describe it. The sheer accumulation of images diminishes the desired effect. It is technically audacious that the narrative itself should prove to be as wild and turbulent as the river, sucking the reader into its maelstrom, but the simulated literary experience is over-saturated. It is a style of narration, like that of yarn spinning, that is enhanced by the celebrated and matchless powers associated with good (and bad) bourbon whiskey.

To be free of the numberless, tiresome inhibitions associated with the choice of words, and their nuances, why not use all of them freely, in fresh combinations, and since the scene is one of disorder, not order, let it begin with the stream of disorderly impressions (we all have them) and a relaxed free-flowing syntax, in which the reader bobs up and down, like an apple: ". . . the water, that innocent-appearing medium [in a flood?] which at one time had held him in iron-like and shifting convolutions like an anaconda"—the writer swept along on his own flood of words, no small feat if it is done for hundreds of pages. There are appreciative echoes of Poe's "Into the Maelstrom" and a nod to Crane's "The Open Boat" in the "arbitrariness of human affairs" that creates such circumstances, while the river that has generated this tempest sweeps author, reader and tale along with it. The reader who snags, or backwaters, or dizzily swirls, or who chokes and goes under, should read something else.

Similar in technique, in the exuberant redundancy of words, in their extravagant application to capture a bizarre, outrageous hallucination, acceptable as an image of grotesque humor or an animated cartoon of comical violence, is this scene from "Spotted Horses":

> A quarter mile further on, the road gashed pallid and moony between the moony shadows of the bordering trees, the horse still galloping, galloping its shadow into the dust, the road descending now toward the creek and the bridge. It was of wood, just wide enough for a single vehicle. When the horse reached it, it was occupied by a wagon coming from the other direction and drawn by two mules already asleep in the harness and the soporific motion. On the seat was Tull and his wife, in splint chairs in the wagon behind them sat their four daughters, all returning belated from an all-day visit with some of Mrs. Tull's kin. The horse neither checked nor swerved. It crashed once on the bridge and rushed between the two mules which waked lunging in opposite directions in the traces, the horse now apparently scrambling along the wagon-tongue itself like a mad squirrel and scrabbling at the end-gate of the wagon with its forefeet as if it intended to climb into the wagon while Tull shouted at it and struck at its face with his whip. The mules were now trying to turn the wagon around in the middle of the bridge. It slewed and tilted, the bridge-rail cracked with a sharp report above the shrieks of the women; the horse scrambled at last across the back of one of the

mules and Tull stood up in the wagon and kicked at its face. Then the front end of the wagon rose, flinging Tull, the reins now wrapped several times about his wrist, backward into the wagon bed among the overturned chairs and the exposed stockings and undergarments of his women. . . . Far up the road now, distancing the frantic mules, the pony faded on. While the five women still shrieked above Tull's unconscious body, Eck and the little boy came up, trotting, Eck still carrying his rope. He was panting. "Which way'd he go?" he said.

The wild humor of this scene, explicit in its exaggeration, is acceptable to the reader as a comic hallucination, the verbal rendering of an event usually reserved for cartoon animation. In his humor Faulkner's rage, his need of and gift for hyperbole, is most at ease with his talent. In the context of frontier humor the bizarre is commonplace, the extravagance enhancing, the lavish rhetoric appropriate to the occasion, the very accumulation of far-fetched images a part of the scene's comic disorder. Imaginations schooled on the two-reel comedies of Mack Sennett, Fatty Arbuckle, Buster Keaton and occasionally Charlie Chaplin would find little unusual in Faulkner's wildest humor except the effort to read him. If read aloud, they would be at ease with his images.

Faulkner is as romantically ready as Fitzgerald, but the surface violence of his landscape effectively conceals the core of sentiment. Behind the extravagant style, beneath the ferment of events, Lena Grove, serene and monumental, makes her way like a sleepwalker through a gothic crackling of passions, radiant in a cloak of impenetrable sentiment.

She begins to eat. She eats slowly, steadily, sucking the rich sardine oil from her fingers with slow and complete relish. Then she stops, not abruptly, yet with utter completeness, her jaw stilled in midchewing, a bitten cracker in her hand and her face lowered a little and her eyes blank, as if she were listening to something very far away or so near as to be inside her. Her face has drained of color, of its full, hearty blood, and she sits quite still, hearing and feeling the implacable and immemorial earth, but without fear or alarm. "It's twins at least," she says to herself, without lip movement, without sound.

Lena Grove is the Great Mother, the abiding earth, the patient and enduring force of life itself, and sentiment saturates Faulkner's image of her. The reason we see her with such empathy, exactly as Faulkner would have us, is because she contrasts so profoundly with the turmoil of lusts, like a "lowering pack of dogs," about to be released. It is this charged atmosphere that gives her serenity such depth, and veils her cloud of sentiment.

The reader swept along on the tide of words and events may hardly be aware that the situation is comic. Faulkner's accumulating rage is kept in bounds—within the scope of the rhetoric—by his humor.

> They were young voices, talking not in shouts or screams but with an unhurried profundity of volume the very apparent absence from which of any discernible human speech or language seemed but natural, as if the sound had been emitted by two enormous birds; as if the aghast and amazed solitude of some inaccessible empty marsh or desert were being invaded and steadily violated by the constant bickering of the last two survivors of a lost species which had established residence in it—a sound which stopped when Ratliff shouted. A moment later the two girls came to the door and stood, big, identical, like two young tremendous cows, looking at him.
>
> "Morning ladies," he said. "Where's your paw?"

A careful reading of this passage suggests that Faulkner writes with his damper wide open, sucking in more air than the occasion warrants—"aghast and amazed solitude of some inaccessible empty marsh"—but without this draft there might have been no fire, only clouds of smoke.

At the heart of this landscape of bizarre disorders and lingering odors, verbena, wisteria and bitches in heat, is a lost paradise, a flowering wilderness, a reservation where violence, the white man's noise, is either kept at bay or laughed out of existence. This landscape glows with the subdued colors appropriate to humor that dissolves rage, and sentiment that dissolves time. There is nothing in literature to compare with the courtship of David Hogganbeck and Ikkemotubbe for Herman Basket's sister, a primal and receding vision of womanliness.

This tale, a stream of clear and undefiled water, winds and unwinds its way through the Faulkner wilderness. It remains pure, where others become corrupt and fouled. It never hurries toward an impending and predictable flood. Hogganbeck and Ikkemotubbe, the eternal dreamers, pursue the mystery of life, the Holy Grail, as it lures them in the form of Herman Basket's sister, the *ewige weibliche* who drew them on and on. She will become the property, predictably, of that colossal ne'er-do-well, Log in the Creek, who lies forever on the floor of the world with his harmonica cupped to his mouth. This vein of mythic humor often erupts in Faulkner, but the reader must be on the alert for it, sunny moments of clearing in a season of thunder, lightning and crackling hail.

As an image-maker, no occasion is too bizarre for the golden touch of Faulkner's imagination.

> . . . Two hours later in the twilight they saw through the streaming windows a burning plantation house. Juxtaposed to nowhere and neighbored by nothing it stood, a clear steady pyre-like flame rigidly fleeing its own reflection, burning in the dusk above the watery desolation with a quality paradoxical, outrageous and bizarre.

"Paradoxical, outrageous and bizarre," evokes the contrary and willful passions that obsess Faulkner's imagination and generate his most memorable visions. In the story "Red Leaves" there is a Negro who has come to the well to drink. "You wanted water," Basket said. "Here it is." The Negro is given a full gourd of water and attempts to drink. They stand watching his throat working, and the bright water cascading down his chin and breast.

> . . . Again they watched his throat working and the unswallowed water sheathing broken and myriad down his chin, channeling his caked chest. They waited, patient, grave, decorous, implacable; clansman and guest and kin. Then the water ceased, though still the empty gourd tilted higher and higher, and still his black throat aped the vain motion of his frustrated swallowing. . . .
>
> "Come," Basket said, taking the gourd from the Negro and hanging it back in the well.

This image of impotence and outrageous frustration gives new life to words that seemed drained of their emotion. Faulkner's thirst-crazed man who can no longer swallow, his throat working while water cascades from his chin, will speak for the writer's and the reader's accumulating frustration and impotent rage.

When dealing with horses and mules, harness, wagons and the man-worn artifacts of rural life, Faulkner is a writer of exact observation, but his inspired images are a blend of literature and imagination. "A Rose for Emily" echoes the macabre visions of Poe.

> The violence of breaking down the door seemed to fill this room with pervading dust. A thin, acrid pall as of the tomb seemed to lie everywhere upon this room decked and furnished as for a bridal: upon the valance curtains of faded rose color, upon the rose-shaded lights, upon the dressing table, upon the delicate array of crystal and the man's toilet things backed with tarnished silver, silver so tarnished that the monogram was obscured. Among them lay a collar and tie, as if they had just been removed, which, lifted, left upon the surface a pale crescent in the dust. Upon a chair hung the suit, carefully folded; beneath it the two mute shoes and discarded socks.

The shoes and socks are Faulkner's touches to the old tableau. An avid reader, he incorporated and expanded on the technical innovations of his contemporaries, in particular the flow and rhythm of the interior monologue, the stream of consciousness, a technique that came so naturally to his gifts we recognize it as the property of the age, the consciousness to which it contributed. In one sustained effort, *The Sound and the Fury*, Faulkner was able to orchestrate the conflicting elements of his nature with his emerging and original gifts as a writer, compressing into a single volume memory, emotion and imagination. The compactness results in a tour de force, a display case of the writer at the top of his form, pulling the stops and sounding the chords that are unmistakably Faulkner. The scene of Luster driving Ben to the left of the monument, not to the right as he was accustomed, causing him to bellow with the shock and horror of all those who fear that the world has taken the wrong way, the wrong turn, forever, is an inspired and unforgettable Faulkner image.

Ben's voice roared and roared. Queenie moved again, her feet began to clop-clop steadily again, and at once Ben hushed. Luster looked quickly back over his shoulder, then he drove on. The broken flower drooped over Ben's fist and his eyes were empty and blue and serene again as cornice and façade flowed smoothly once more from left to right; post and tree, window and doorway, and signboard, each in its ordered place.

# Ernest Hemingway

We passed through a town and stopped in front of the posada, and the driver took on several packages. Then we started on again, and outside the town the road commenced to mount. We were going through farming country with rocky hills that sloped down into the fields. The grain-fields went up the hillsides. Now as we went higher there was a wind blowing the grain. The road was white and dusty, and the dust rose under the wheels and hung in the air behind us. The road climbed up into the hills and left the rich grain-fields below. Now there were only patches of grain on the bare hillsides and on each side of the water-courses.

The impersonal tone of this narration is a highly personal glimpse into the narrator. His reserve has *style*. The use of "now" evokes presence and immediacy. The language is simple enough, but in the word repetitions, in the pacing of the phrases, the contrast of the long and short sentences, the writer deliberately appeals to the senses, both to what is seen and how it sounds to the ear. Only talent will explain why this style of narration captivated and enthralled a generation of writers and readers. We can assume they all coveted the posture of the cool, capable but secretly vulnerable exile. The music of the style owes much to Gertrude Stein, which it was part of his talent to recognize and purloin, thereby inhibiting, by his example, her own experiments with language. Nor

141

would style alone have captured the literate public. The deeper, irresistible appeal is the presence in the writing of what is most personal to the writer.

> If I could have made this enough of a book it would have had everything in it. The Prado, looking like some big American college building, with sprinklers watering the grass early in the bright Madrid summer morning; the bare white mud hills looking across toward Carabanchel; days on the train in August with the blinds pulled down on the side against the sun and the wind blowing them; the chaff blown against the car in the wind from the hard earthen threshing floors; the odor of grain and the stone windmills.

This is Hemingway in Spain (*Death in the Afternoon*). It is not fiction but the style is the same, and projects the same persona. The eye of memory he casts back on his experience burns and glances off the sun-baked surface, like that of a scanning camera, yet it captures the emotion invisible to the camera. This is the art of it, the secret to the style, the siren voice that lures the reader to possess the experience and write about it *in this manner*. The manner is crucial. The author believes this, and is always at pains to talk, write and live in this style. The reader believes this, and is at pains, through absorbing this style, to possess the experience. When applied to a place, an event or a woman, the style simulates possession.

> . . . I know things change now and I do not care. It's all been changed for me. Let it all change. We'll all be gone before it's changed too much and if no deluge comes when we are gone it will still rain in summer in the north and hawks will nest in the Cathedral at Santiago and in La Granja, where we practiced with the cape on the long gravelled paths between the shadows, it makes no difference if the fountains play or not. We never will ride back from Toledo in the dark, washing the dust out with Fundador, nor will there be that week of what happened in the night in that July in Madrid. We've seen it all go and we'll watch it go again. The great thing is to last and to get your work done and see and hear and learn and understand; and write when there is something that you know; and not before; and not too damned much after.

Both Fitzgerald and Hemingway, in their contrasting voices, chronicle the same downward path to wisdom, the resignation of the American man-child turning thirty, the dark fields of the republic, the dun-colored mountains of Spain, forever and ever receding behind them. The soliloquy of Hemingway is more manly in its resignation, but no longer conceals, as it once seemed to, the prodigal saying goodbye to his youth. The sentiments are heightened, the emotions are swayed by the musical play of light and shadow, of hawks and fountains, of dust, Fundador and whatever happened that night in Madrid, better left unmentioned now that it is gone. Readers who had little notion of work to be done, and writers who had little talent for lasting, were never quite the same after reading this passage, or free of its romantic and haunting renunciation. We'll to the woods no more: *les lauriers sont coupés.*

Hemingway has few equals in the emotion he is able to evoke from the surface of an image. It is often in passing, before the mind's eye of memory, or from the window of a train or a moving car, a *series of images* being important, each one reduced to the power of a symbol—light and shadow, hawk and fountain, rain in summer—which he orchestrates for the desired effect.

> What about the ranch and the silvered gray of the sage brush, the quick, clear water in the irrigation ditches, and the heavy green of the alfalfa. The trail went up into the hills and the cattle in the summer were shy as deer. The bawling and the steady noise and slow moving mass raising a dust as you brought them down in the fall. And behind the mountains, the clear sharpness of the peak in the evening light and, riding down along the trail in the moonlight, bright across the valley. Now he remembered coming through the timber in the dark holding the horse's tail when you could not see and all the stories that he meant to write.

Not France, not Spain, but the ranch in the West evoked in the same hypnotic rhythms a similar flow of impressions, the use of "now" to enhance immediacy, suggesting a moving panorama, as if these scenes were painted on a canvas that unrolled before him, cinematic in quality. The stream-of-consciousness technique has been adapted to the fluency of narration. Without apparent strain, as if it came naturally, the writer incorporates the innovations of the decade into an artlessly flowing vernacular style. The flow of this style calls for a dialogue that is in sharp contrast, cryptic and laconic.

"How do you feel?" she said. She had come out from the tent now after her bath.

"All right."

"Could you eat now?" He saw Molo behind her with the folding table and the other boy with the dishes.

"I want to write," he said.

"You ought to take some broth to keep your strength up."

"I'm going to die tonight," he said. "I don't need my strength up."

"Don't be melodramatic, Harry, please," she said.

Lyrically flowing, poetically sensitive narration contrasts perfectly with the hard-boiled dialogue. Hemingway sensed and provided the formula for the public-private sectors of American life, the tough exteriors, the sensitive, brooding interiors, spawning the macho-tough fiction and the Bogart movies.

When the tautness of the Hemingway line slackens, the words in the line lose their charge of emotion, hang like limp sails. The cinematic flow of images is displaced with a series of static stills, connected by "then" and "and."

They went under the white bridge and under the unfinished wood bridge. Then they left the red bridge on the right and passed under the first high-flying white bridge. Then there was the black iron fret-work bridge on the canal leading into the Rio Nuovo and they passed the two stakes chained together but not touching: like us the Colonel thought.

The formula is operative here: we recognize the hand of the potter, but without the usual charge of emotion it seems a retarded impression, like that of Faulkner's Benjy in *The Sound and the Fury*. The images are inert, the repetitions horizontal rather than flowing, the words drained of the energy that once made them vibrant. They are now *signs*, and please only the reader who remembers them as symbols and treasures the style for its nostalgia as the Colonel treasures Venice.

> Christ, I love it, he said, and I'm so happy I helped defend it when I was a punk kid, and with an insufficient command of the language and I never even saw her until that clear day in the winter when I went back to have that small wound dressed, and saw her rising from the sea.

This is self-parody, pitiless as the scorn Hemingway so freely applied to those who displeased him. *Across the River and into the Trees* is a writer's manual of the treacheries of a great "style." The music that once held the reader now captivates the author. He can hear nothing else. The author's first mistake was to return to the scene of an early, image-making triumph. Time has not displaced that experience. The tremors of emotion felt by the Colonel are not communicated to the reader. An old lover, in a gondola, warming himself with his own clichés. About Spain he had written:

> . . . Pamplona is changed, of course, but not as much as we are older. I found that if you took a drink that it got very much the same as it was always.

For the drinker, perhaps, but not for the reader. If this writer is to escape from his own fiction, he must find new objects of affection, of attachment. *Islands in the Stream,* published posthumously, finds him at ease with sentiment, indulgent with humor and admitting of binding ties with a cat named Boise.

> One time on the Central Highway he had seen a cat that had been hit by a car and the cat, fresh hit and dead, looked exactly like Boy [his own cat]. . . . He knew it couldn't be Boy . . . but it had made him feel sick inside and he had stopped the car and gone back and lifted the cat and made sure it was not Boy and then laid him by the side of the road so nothing else would run over him. . .
> That evening, coming back to the farm, the body of the cat was gone from where he had left him so he thought that his people

must have found him. That night, when he had sat in the big chair reading, with Boise by his side in the chair, he had thought that he did not know what he would do if Boise should be killed. He thought, from his actions and his desperations, that the cat felt the same way about the man.

There is neither sarcasm nor manly detachment in this admission of sentiment, of vulnerability. The truly binding ties are merely there to be acknowledged, rather than challenged, mocked or explained.

In Thomas Hudson, the central figure of the novel, we have a self-portrait that contradicts the familiar, long-standing re-presentation, the hunter, the warrior, the public figure and self-approving, if tormented, creator. For a brief moment, in the shelter of the sun and sea at his home in Cuba, he seemed free of the destructive obsessions, the increasing paranoia, that determined his public image. Although *The Old Man and the Sea* is in the mannered and celebrated style that inhibits more than it releases, it provides the parable for Hemingway's vision of life as a losing battle, over which style, courage and tenacity triumph.

As the gifts of age crowned his lifetime's effort, the last losing battle of his life found him in the role of both the hunter and the hunted, a theme that would have challenged him more profoundly than the bullrings of Spain, or the green hills of Africa. How well he had come to know each protagonist! Romantically ready, predictably disenchanted, the postwar writers were committed to heroics that excluded the possibility of growing old. They shared the expectations that made them vulnerable and unmistakably American. The old man of the sea, of Pamplona, of Kilimanjaro, whom we see bearded and brooding in Karsh's portrait, is still the youth cleaning his trout on the banks of the Big Two-hearted River. He had found that if you took a drink it had got very much as it was always. The way alcohol has fueled and prematurely depleted the gifts Americans reserve for the highest calling suggests that the brook between youth and age has long been too broad for leaping. Falling into it had become the heroic way of life.

# Richard Wright: Real and Imagined Black Voices

Does the writer's "voice" have a color? Or is its pigmentation a property of the language, explicit as a sign or a gesture, signifying black. The American vernacular confers on the writer a choice of pigmentations.

> "I was a listenin' to all de talk, en I slips into de river and was gwyne to shove for sho if de come aboard. Den I was gwyne to swim to de raf agin when de was gone."

> "I uz settn' down front er de fireplace," she said, "cookn' some meat, w'en all of a sudden I year sumpin at de do'—scratch, scratch. I tuck'n tun de meat over, en make out I aint year it. Bimeby it come dar 'gin—scratch, scratch."

> "I hears you," Dilsey said. "All I been hearin, when you in de house. Ef hit aint Quentin or yo maw, hit's Luster en Benjy. Whut you let him go on dat way fer, Miss Cahline?"

The first voice is that of Mark Twain, speaking through Jim, the second Joel Chandler Harris, speaking through Lucinda, the third Faulkner speaking through Dilsey. Each writer improvises his own impression of black speech, feelings, and thought rhythms. In Gertrude Stein's "Melanctha" it is the writer's talent that gives the voice its authenticity.

147

Sometimes the thought of how all her world was made filled the complex, desiring Melanctha with despair. She wondered, often, how she could go on living when she was so blue.

In *Cane,* the black writer Jean Toomer minimizes the clichés of black vernacular thought.

Dorris: Nothin doin? How come? Aint I as good as him? Couldnt I have got an education if I'd wanted one? Dont I know respectable folks, lots of em, in Philadelphia and New York and Chicago? Aint I had men as good as him? Better. Doctors an lawyers. Whats a manager's brother, anyhow?

In the main he speaks with his own voice:

Her soul is like a little thrust-tailed dog that follows her, whimpering.

A few years younger than Toomer, Zora Neale Hurston had the benefit of his example. In *Their Eyes Were Watching God,* she combines the picturesque gusto of black vernacular speech with a somber and evocative prose lyricism.

Ships at a distance have every man's wish on board. For some they come in with the tide. For others they sail forever on the horizon, never out of sight, never landing until the Watcher turns his eyes away in resignation, his dreams mocked to death by Time. That is the life of men.

This distillation owes more to oral than written tradition, and it is this fund of folk wisdom that gives it substance and authority. It is not the writer's personal "voice" but one of the tongues of men that speak through her. We are closer to her own inimitable style in this passage:

She was stretched on her back beneath the pear tree soaking in the alto chant of the visiting bees, the gold of the sun and the panting breath of the breeze when the inaudible voice of it all came to her. She saw a dust-bearing bee sink into the sanctum of a bloom; the thousand sister-calyxes arch to meet the love embrace and the ecstatic shiver of the tree from root to tiniest branch creaming in every blossom and frothing with delight.

This refinement of sensation is not possible in the public theatre of dialect. Other things, are, however—

> "Dey all useter call me Alphabet 'cause so many people had done named me different names. Ah looked at de picture a long time and seen it was mah dress and mah hair so Ah said:
> " 'Aw, aw! Ah'm colored!'
> "Den dey all laughed real hard. But before Ah seen de picture Ah thought Ah wuz just like de rest."

The bold contrast of these two voices gives the story an enhanced public and private dimension. It has a day and a night side to its being. The bubbling vitality of the street talk is the play and sparkle of light on the surface of deeper waters. Both Toomer and Hurston are closer to Stein than the fashionable vernacular of Porgy and Bess, soon to flower in the theatre of Amos & Andy. Each writer's nature has been shaped by experience, but each has learned to write from what he has read. In *The Fire Next Time* James Baldwin speaks for himself:

> But I cannot leave it at that; there is more to it than that. In spite of everything, there was in the life I fled a zest and a joy and a capacity for facing and surviving disaster that are very moving and very rare. Perhaps we were, all of us—pimps, whores, racketeers, church members, and children—bound together by the nature of our oppression, the specific and peculiar complex of risks we had to run; if so, within these limits we sometimes achieved with each other a freedom that was close to love.

This language has no color: what it has is the tone of a cultivated and accomplished writer, at ease in the language of his choice. He has learned to write by reading the best writing, most of it by whites. Ralph Ellison's *Invisible Man* is also careful to avoid explicit color connotations.

> I am an invisible man. No, I am not a spook like those who haunted Edgar Allan Poe; nor am I one of your Hollywood-movie ectoplasms. I am a man of substance, of flesh and bone, fiber and liquids—and I might even be said to possess a mind I am

invisible, understand, simply because people refuse to see me.

He does not say white people. Few would guess from this statement that the speaker is black. The sophisticated tone and resonance of the narration echoes both European and American examples, but reveals no color bias. The author is first of all a writer, and his work takes such color as it has from writing.

Richard Wright is visibly and unmistakably black, but it is not self-evident in his style. A loner among loners, his voice is distinguished by its uncompromising honesty and candor.

> . . . Men hate themselves and it makes them hate others . . . We must find some way of being good to ourselves . . . Man is all we've got . . . I wish I could ask men to meet themselves . . . We're different from what we seem . . . Maybe worse, maybe better . . . But certainly different . . . We're strangers to ourselves.

This writer has a soul brother in Camus, but he has not found the brotherhood he seeks in exile. An early admirer of Stein's "Melanctha," Wright understandably had some misgivings of such a white woman's knowledge of black experience. It had led him to read the story to black stockyard workers, to test its vernacular and speech rhythms on non-sophisticated listeners. They had been enthralled. Talent, not color, endowed the writer with an authentic voice. Wright's voice, like Faulkner's, derives its conviction and power from the charge of his emotions, the sustained fury of rage for justice.

> I read Dreiser's *Jennie Gerhardt* and *Sister Carrie* and they revived in me a vivid sense of my mother's suffering; I was overwhelmed. I grew silent, wondering about the life around me. It would have been impossible for me to have told anyone what I derived from these novels, for it was nothing less than a sense of life itself. All my life had shaped me for the realism, the naturalism of the modern novel, and I could not read enough of them.

After Dreiser, Wright is one of the few writers of power and substance to find the tents of naturalism congenial. If it had not existed, Wright would of necessity have been its founder. The passionate struggle for survival, as spelled out by Darwin, was explicitly true of his own experience. Likewise the writings of Marx, explaining that social forces, not race or color, determined the lives of most people. These complex, heady, revolutionary assumptions fit the facts of his life, and added fuel to his talent. The problems of the novel that intrigued other writers—those of form, of style, of innovation—were peripheral to his interests. He knew about them, he often thought about them, but the nature of his experience, and the demands of his nature, had little use for them. Life *was* a battle. How keep it out of his books? Compared with the heat of Wright's anger, Faulkner's impotent rage was distantly romantic, a gothic outrage indulgently remembered. Wright was helpless, but not impotent—a crucial element of rhetorical violence. Wright personifies the figure of the lynched man who refuses to be cut down or silenced.

> My mother's suffering grew into a symbol in my mind gathering to itself all the poverty, the ignorance, the helplessness; the painful baffling, hunger-ridden days and hours; the restless moving, the futile seeking, the uncertainty, the fear, the dread; the meaningless pain and the endless suffering. . . . A somberness of spirit that I was never to lose settled over me during the slow years of my mother's unrelieved suffering, a somberness that was to make me stand apart and look upon excessive joy with suspicion, that was to make me self-conscious, that was to make me keep forever on the move, as though to escape a nameless fate seeking to overtake me.

This rage to live will not be silenced. Intelligent, fearless, brutally honest, striking out at black and white injustices alike, Wright speaks for a state of grace appropriate to a noble but threatened savage trapped in an increasingly alien wilderness. Forever on the move, he goes to Paris, for such comforts as he can find in exile, but this escape from what he finds intolerable at home has its price. The native son, black or white, who is driven or hounded from his homeland is the one, of all of nature's orphaned children, who cannot live fully without it. It is *his* land, in the fullness of its promise, as it is never actually possessed by those who live insensibly at peace within it.

> At the age of twelve, before I had had one full year of formal schooling, I had a conception of life that no experience would ever erase, a predilection for what was real that no argument would ever gainsay, a sense of the world that was mine and mine alone, a notion as to what life meant that no education would ever alter, a conviction that the meaning of life came only when one was struggling to wring a meaning out of meaningless suffering.

In these passages from *Black Boy*, a record of childhood and youth, where Wright is speaking of himself, and for himself, we are persuaded to believe what he tells us and accept his impression of the world around him.

> Though I had long known that there were people called "white" people, it had never meant anything to me emotionally. I had seen white men and women upon the streets a thousand times, but they never looked particularly "white." To me they were merely people like other people, yet somehow strangely different since I had never come in close touch with any of them. For the most part I never thought of them; they simply existed somewhere in the background of the city as a whole. It might have been that my tardiness in learning to sense white people as "white" people came from the fact that many of my relatives were "white"-looking people. My grandmother, who was white as any "white" person, had never looked "white" to me.

This rings true to life, and true to this writer. In his fiction, however, where the emotions and happenings of his life are projected onto others, the overall effect is diminished. This apparent contradiction of the facts is one of the craft problems of fiction. Wright's accumulating rage needs no justification, but if it leads to overkill it impairs the fiction and alienates the reader. Applied psychology takes the place of direct reporting and harrowing emotion.

> His memory of his relationship with Dot was not only a recollection of a man's sensual affair with a pretty girl he had forsaken in the trouble he had brought on her; but above all, Dot

had been to him a representation of a personal hunger which he had projected out of his heart on her, and the two of them—Dot and what she subjectively meant to him—had been something he had not been able to cope with with satisfaction to himself and honor to her.

This is the tone of narration used by Cross in Wright's novel *The Outsider*. Applied psychology has watered emotion: a projected "representation of personal hunger" is a far remove from the author's experience. For most writers some remove is necessary, a fictive distance that permits an objective re-creation, an enlargement and enhancement, but for Wright this assumed detachment dilutes his anger and betrays his experience. It is the "I," the intimate voice of the writer, that gives energy and conviction to his writing. The complex and necessary artifices of the novel come between the writer, his memories and his emotion. Shared by so many characters, the emotion is depleted, the words are often drained of conviction. Wright had surely read the French writer Céline, and he might have taken a hint from his example. His long *Journey to the End of the Night* is resolutely in the first person singular. The writer consumed with a smoldering rage is not at his best when re-creating others. Predictably perhaps, for a man of Wright's nature and experience, exile in Paris did not freshly arouse his abiding anger, or lead to new writing interests. Although spared further painful humiliations, he had become an outsider in both cultures. The tolerance of those who do not see you at all can prove to be more galling than those who see only your color. His true and indispensable life was still back where he had left it.

I was in my fifteenth year; in terms of schooling I was far behind the average youth of the nation, but I did not know that. In me was shaping a yearning for a kind of consciousness, a mode of being that the way of life about me had said could not be, must not be, and upon which the penalty of death had been placed. Somewhere in the dead of the southern night my life had switched on to the wrong track and, without my knowing it, the locomotive of my heart was rushing down a dangerously steep slope, heading for collision, heedless of the warning red lights that blinked all about me, the sirens and the bells and the screams that filled the air.

These closing words echo a tune heard (of all places) in the enlarged and doomed heart of Jay Gatsby, testifying as nothing else (unless it's the whisper of the trombones, the ghostly rumble of the drums) to what is incurable in the plight of our native sons.

# James Agee

Occasionally overwrought, consistently overwhelming, Agee's *Let Us Now Praise Famous Men* narrows the gap between the observer and what he observes. Words have seldom received such a charge of emotion to no other end than a reverence for life. The book is a long, extended devotion, unfaltering in its power to praise what exists. Revelation on this scale is embarrassing, and many readers find the book intolerably poignant. The ideal form for this passion would have been music, a pure and soaring aria of emotion, but he was a writer so uniquely endowed the words evoke the unheard music. In the craft of image-making this calls for new vibrations from old chords:

By now three others stood in the outskirts who had been sent for by a running child; they were young men, only twenty to thirty, yet very old and sedate; and their skin was of that sootiest black which no light can make shine and with which the teeth are blue and the eyeballs gold. They wore pressed trousers, washed shoes, brilliantly starched white shirts, bright ties, and carried newly whited straw hats in their hands, and at their hearts were pinned the purple and gilded ribbons of a religious and burial society. They had been summoned to sing for Walker and for me, to show us what nigger music is like (though we had done all we felt we were able to spare them and ourselves this summons), and they stood patiently in a stiff frieze in the oak shade, their hats and their shirts shedding light, and were waiting to be noticed and released, for they had been on their way to church when the child caught them; and now that they were looked at and the order given they stepped forward a few paces, not smiling, and stopped in rigid line, and, after a constricted exchange of glances among themselves, the eldest tapping the clean dirt with his shoe, they sang.

This is early in the book, and both prepares and warns the reader. The writer's powers of description are difficult to appreciate without sharing his torment.

> . . . [the music] tore itself like a dance of sped plants out of three young men who stood sunk to their throats in land, and whose eyes were neither shut nor looking at anything; the screeching young tenor, the baritone, stridulant in the height of his register, his throat tight as a fist, and the bass, rolling the iron wheels of his machinery, his hand clenching and loosening as he tightened and relaxed against the spraining of his ellipses: and they were abruptly silent; totally wooden; while the landowner smiled coldly.

In a word to the reader the author says:

> If I could do it, I'd do no writing at all here. It would be photographs; the rest would be fragments of cloth, bits of cotton, lumps of earth, records of speech, pieces of wood and iron, phials of odors, plates of food and of excrement.

This point is well taken. He wants to emphasize that these objects *exist:* they are not mere words or phantoms of his imagination. A reverence for life, for facts, for existentials dictates this honorable admission. The photographs of Walker Evans that accompany the volume memorably confirm their actual existence. The writer who would do no writing at all proceeds to write another five hundred pages. In such fashion do we acknowledge that what exists does not speak for itself.

But whether the image is imagined or taken hot from life, his own eyes the lens of the camera, once the writer would put that impression into words he is a good, or a bad, writer of fiction, a maker of images.

> ... skin of that sootiest black which no light can make shine and with which the teeth are blue and the eyeballs gold ...

> ... jagged, tortured, stony, accented as if by hammers and cold chisels ... the harmonies constantly splitting the nerves ...

> ... it tore itself like a dance of sped plants out of three young men who stood sunk to their throats in land ...

> ... the bass, rolling the iron wheels of his machinery, his hand clenching and loosening as he tightened and relaxed against the spraining of his ellipses ...

These images involve all of our senses, of which the visible is but one aspect. A photograph of these young men, one by Walker Evans, would seize on a decisive revelatory moment in a manner that shames and silences comment, but the writer is able to expand and amplify on that visual impression to create a new and more complex image. We don't see it all. We seldom see more than what we know.

The ineluctably visible is the obsession of our time, and the camera is its unique instrument, but within and behind what is visible are the "spraining ellipses" of consciousness. The actual is ineffable, but for the maker of images it is merely a point of departure.

> A small octagonal frame surfaced in ivory and black ribbons of thin wicker or of straw, the glass broken out: set in this frame, not filling it, a fading box-camera snapshot: low, gray, dead-looking land stretched back in a deep horizon; twenty yards back, one corner of a tenant house, central at the foreground, two women: Annie Mae's sister Emma as a girl of twelve, in slippers and stockings and a Sunday dress, standing a little shyly with puzzling eyes, self-conscious of her appearance and of her softly clouded sex; and their mother, wide and high, in a Sunday dress still wet from housework, her large hands hung loose and biased in against her thighs, her bearing strong, weary, and noble, her face fainted away almost beyond distinguishing, as if in her death and by some

secret touching the image itself of the fine head her husband had
cared for so well had softly withered, which even while they stood
there had begun its blossoming inheritance in the young daughter
at her side.

As this passage closes, the charge of emotion strains the
image, as if rippled by heat. The figures are so "real" to us we
are startled to be reminded that her face has lost its distinguishing features. All pictures are open to "interpretation,"
and without captions most photographs make ambiguous statements. The observer is challenged to make his own judgment.
This snapshot that speaks so poignantly to Agee might hold
little interest for the reader. He has seen countless pictures.
Each of them—so he has been told—speaking louder than
words. The proliferation of "images" that we now take for
granted, in magazines, newspapers, the TV, the movies, has so
diminished the image's impact that it has lost much of its
power as "representation." We see it as a picture, a piece of
picture-making. In the snapshot just described a filter would
have helped, a better lens would have picked up missing
details. But what camera would have captured Emma's softly
clouded sex? Agee's word picture is detailed and vibrant in a
way that exceeds the lens of the camera. Rather than a
description, or a translation, it is a new, irreplaceable image.

> . . . I told Ricketts how sorry we had been the way it had turned
> out awhile back, getting her and the children all lined up and
> taking pictures without giving her any explanation, and keeping
> them all from their dinners, and he said she didn't keer nothn
> about none of that, in a tone which without unkindness meant
> that she didn't have a right to, so if she did it made no difference.
> I told him I couldn't be a bit sure yet just where our work was
> going to be taking us, but I hoped we would be seeing them all
> some more. He said, any time, they were always right there, then
> he said, any time, they were always right there. Then he laughed
> very loudly and said, yes sir, any time at all, they was sure God
> always right there. Then he laughed very loud and long and said,
> yes sir, they was always right there all right, any time at all, and

kept on laughing while, out of the back of his eyes, he watched me. That is the pattern of almost anything Ricketts says.

The images of Agee aspire to be icons accessible to worship and prayerful release. Some are devotions, invoking silence, or ceremonial genuflections. His purpose is liturgical, to exalt in a ritual of purification. In the vernacular sense, Agee is a "religious," one inspired to provide his own holy writ, and the exposure of such emotions disturbs and embarrasses some readers.

> ... I do not make myself welcome here. My whole flesh; my whole being; is withdrawn upon nothingness. Not even so much am I here as, last night, in the dialogue of those two creatures of darkness. What is taking place here, and it happens daily in this silence, is intimately transacted between this home and eternal space; and consciousness has no residence in nor pertinence to it save only that, privileged by stealth to behold, we fear this legend: withdraw; bow down; nor dare the pride to seek to decipher it. ...

In this passage the intended elevation has thinned the air, and we hear the writer panting. As he adjusts to it, he goes on:

> At this certain time of late morning, then, in the full breadth of summer, here in this dark and shuttered room, through a knothole near the sharp crest of the roof, a signal or designation is made each day in silence and unheeded. A long bright rod of light takes to its end, on the left side of the mantel, one of the small vases of milky and opalescent glass; in such a way, through its throat, and touching nothing else, that from within its self this tholed phial glows its whole shape on the obscurity, a sober grail, or divinity local to this home; and no one watches it, this archaic form, and alabastrine pearl, and captured paring of the phosphor moon, in what inhuman piety and silent fear it shows: and after a half minute it is faded and is changed, and is only a vase with a light on it, companion of a never-lighted twin, and they stand in wide balance on the narrow shelf;

So this place is a tabernacle, this mantel is an altar, and we are in the presence of hallowed objects, and a chosen moment appropriate to worship. It is surely epiphanal to the writer, but may overextend the responses of the reader. One misses the swinging censers, the signs, the genuflections, but accepts their presence by implication. "Alabastrine pearl" and "phosphor moon" symbolize the state of soul being evoked. The reader familiar with liturgical observance will more readily identify with the emotion Agee invests in these objects.

Is there a connection, however unlikely in appearance, between the exaltation Agee seeks and finds in this ceremony and that sought and found by Fitzgerald in the "passion" of Gatsby, his gift of hope, his romantic readiness? Fitzgerald's emotions are often self-serving, self-immolating; he is often his own sacrificial offering, but his inscrutable purpose is transcendent. He wanted nothing less than the impossible. He is exact when he uses the word "ecstasy" to describe his sensations. These profoundly different men, so opposed in their practice, were alike in their desire to walk on water and drink the milk of paradise. Each stretched the filament of great expectations to an incandescent glow.

> All over Alabama, the lamps are out. Every leaf drenches the touch; the spider's net is heavy. The roads lie there, with nothing to use them. The fields lie there, with nothing at work in them, neither man nor beast. The plow handles are wet, and the rails and the frogplates and the weeds between the ties: and not even the hurryings and hoarse sorrows of a distant train, on other roads, is heard.

Why should the gift of hope enhance the holiness of poverty? In the presence of impaired and ravaged lives, Agee is as prostrate on the clay soil of Alabama as Fitzgerald on the "bright tan prayer rug" of the Riviera. The simplest of human actualities provokes Agee to a somber, lyrical, transcendent imagery, at once grave, earthbound and soaring.

> . . . His dress has fallen aside and he is naked. As he is held, the head huge in scale of his body, the small body ineffably relaxed, spilled in a deep curve from nape to buttocks, then the knees drawn up a little, the bottom small and sharp, and the legs and

feet drifted as if under water, he suggests the shape of the word siphon. He is nursing. His hands are blundering at her breast blindly, as if themselves each were a new born creature, or as if they were sobbing, ecstatic with love; his mouth is intensely absorbed at her nipple as if in rapid kisses, with small and swift sounds of moisture; his eyes are squeezed shut; and now, for breath, he draws away, and lets out a sharp short whispered *ahh*, the hands and his eyelids relaxing, and immediately resumes; and in all this while, his face is beatific, the face of one at rest in paradise, and in all this while her gentle and sober, earnest face is not altered out of its deep slantwise gazing: his head is now sunken off and away, grand and soft as a cloud, his wet mouth flared, his body still more profoundly relinquished of itself, and I see how against her body he is so many things in one, the child in the melodies of the womb, the Madonna's son, human divinity sunken from the cross at rest against his mother, and more beside, for at the heart and leverage of that young body, gently, taken in all the pulse of his being, the penis is partly erected.

This writer is unsurpassed in his power to sense and explore a reverence for life that is at once earthbound and transcendent. The mystic meaning proper to the commonplace provokes him to recognition and revelation, a poet who is called to make manifest what is usually concealed. The true reader of Agee is compelled, as in an act of communion, to an expansion of consciousness.

# Carson McCullers

> In the town there were two mutes, and they were always together.

This simple image, the opening line of the novel, arrests the reader's attention. He must pause and reconsider what he has read. Two mutes, who are always together. It could not be more simply stated, but the image evoked is provocative. The word "mute" has a new resonance in this context. The tone is formal and detached, like the opening of a fable:

> ... Early every morning they would come out from the house where they lived and walk arm in arm down the street to work. The two friends were very different. The one who always steered the way was an obese and dreamy Greek. In the summer he would come out wearing a yellow or green polo shirt stuffed sloppily into his trousers in front and hanging loose behind. When it was colder he wore over this a shapeless gray sweater. His face was round and oily, with half-closed eyelids and lips that curved in a gentle, stupid smile. The other mute was tall. His eyes had a quick, intelligent expression. He was always immaculate and very soberly dressed.

The detached tone of narration, the explicit detail of the tableau, chimes with that of another youthful writer, describing a battle he had never seen:

> The cold passed reluctantly from the earth, and the retiring fogs revealed an army stretched out on the hills, resting.

These opening lines challenge both writers to sustain the effect they have made on the reader. The language is exact, as if both writers are at pains to describe what they actually see. Invisible, but present, is the emotion of the writer as the lines are shaped to his purpose. The words are plain enough, but "the cold that passes reluctantly from the earth" is an uncommon image. It is the author's purpose to shape the reader, as well as the line. Where style is present, its recognition will entice one reader more than another. Readers of Crane will take easily to Carson McCullers, who shares with him a gift for the telling, the audacious image. *The Heart Is a Lonely Hunter* is a long novel, but our first impression of the two mutes will prove to be the memorable one. The poetic truth lies in the image, not the demonstration. Crane, O'Connor and McCullers create images that are touched with a sense of the Orphic, of commonplace yet mysterious revelation. We feel it to be of a different order from what we consider normal. Tone is crucial to this effect, as it would be in the voice of an oracle, or a soothsayer. We receive this impression without question. The voice is at once detached and omniscient.

> . . . There is a fort in the South where a few years ago a murder was committed. The participants of this tragedy were: two officers, a soldier, two women, a Filipino, and a horse.

The flat recounting of this information leaves little room for speculation. The reader also senses that the story that follows will exceed these facts. *Reflections in a Golden Eye* is a short novel, with a minimum of psychological probing.

> On the post Leonora Penderton enjoyed a reputation as a good hostess, an excellent sportswoman, and even as a great lady. However, there was something about her that puzzled her friends and acquaintances. They sensed an element in her personality that they could not quite put their fingers on. The truth of the matter was that she was a little feeble-minded.

How right it seems when we read it. But we are offered no clue as to how the narrating voice has come by this knowledge. The charm of such a style, and the persuasion of such a voice, is that we accept what we read without question: our habitual disbelief is in suspension.

This posture of detachment, of authorial distance, is ill suited for fiction that solicits the reader's personal involvement. In *The Member of the Wedding* that same writer has the use of a different voice.

> Frances wanted the whole world to die. . . . She was sitting next to Berenice, back with the colored people, and when she thought of it she used the mean word she had never used before, nigger— for now she hated everyone and wanted only to spite and shame. For John Henry West the wedding had only been a great big show, and he had enjoyed her misery at the end as he had enjoyed the angel cake. She mortally despised him, dressed in his best white suit, now stained with strawberry ice cream. Berenice she hated also, for to her it had only meant a pleasure trip to Winter Hill. Her father, who had said that he would attend to her when they got home, she would like to kill. She was against every single person, even strangers in the crowded bus, though she only saw them blurred by tears—and she wished the bus would fall in a river or run into a train. Herself she hated worst of all, and she wanted the whole world to die.

Most readers will identify with Frances, since they have felt such sorrow and hurt themselves, and know that, deep down, she doesn't really mean it, and likes the world more than she hates it. It is through this knowledge, intimately shared with the reader, that the voice shamelessly appeals for understanding, knowing that this reader will prove to be sympathetic. This is a triumph of the personal, the openly vulnerable and sentimental (the voice that speaks for the young and not as yet disillusioned), in contrast to the omniscient and impersonal voice of *Reflections in a Golden Eye*. It is rare that a writer is equally at ease in such opposing styles. The adult world is either filtered through the eyes of the young, silently mirrored in the eyes of a mute or refracted in the gold-brown eyes of Private Williams. He, too, is mutelike. For such characters to speak reduces their mystery.

> . . . he kept his grave, deep gaze on the Captain's wife. The expression of his mute face had not been changed by his experience, but now and then he narrowed his gold-brown eyes as though he were forming within himself some subtle scheme . . . The light behind him laid a great dim shadow of himself on the smooth grass of the lawn. The soldier walked like a man weighted by a dark dream and his footsteps were soundless.

Having gazed upon Leonora, naked, the soldier is captive of a nameless longing. Predictably he is a loner, subject to fantasies, and his closest companion is a horse.

> . . . His horse was an ordinary army plug which, with anyone but Private Williams, could sustain only two gaits—a clumsy trot and a rocking-horse gallop. But with the soldier a marvelous change came over the animal; he cantered or single-footed with proud, stiff elegance. The soldier's body was of a pale golden brown and he held himself erect. Without his clothes he was so slim that the pure, curved outlines of his ribs could be seen. As he cantered about in the sunlight, there was a sensual, savage smile on his lips that would have surprised his barrack mates. After such outings he came back weary to the stables and spoke to no one.

Leonora's husband, Captain Penderton, is tantalized and troubled by the thought of the soldier.

> . . . During their brief, impersonal meetings he suffered a curious lapse of sensory impressions; when he was near the soldier he found himself unable to see or to hear properly . . . The thought of the young man's face—the dumb eyes, the heavy sensual lips that were often wet, the childish page-boy bangs—this image was intolerable to him . . . the sound of his slurring Southern voice meandered constantly in the back of his mind like a troubling song.

This is as explicit as the narrator becomes in suggesting the Captains's doomed attraction. His struggle with his unmentionable temptation parallels the soldier's passion for the

Captain's wife. They both live with a desire that smolders and increases, but remains unadmitted.

> The Captain . . . knew that the soldier must now realize that these afternoon walks were made on his account. It even occurred to the Captain to wonder why the soldier did not evade him and go elsewhere at this time. The fact that the soldier clung to his habit gave to these daily contacts a flavor of assignation that filled the Captain with excitement. After he had passed the soldier he had to suppress a craving to turn around, and as he walked away he felt his heart swell with a wild, nostalgic sadness which he could not control.

Like the soldier, the Captain appears to suffer from an affliction that he cannot help. The situation is bizarre, but it remains convincing through absence of actual confrontations, and explicitly homosexual comments. Both men are possessed by their passions, as if drugged. The physical confrontation is not between the two men, or the soldier and the woman, but between the Captain and the horse.

> . . . Slowly and methodically he tied the horse to a tree. He broke off a long switch and with the last of his spent strength began to beat the horse savagely. Breathing in great gasps, his coat dark and curled with sweat, the horse at first moved restively about the tree. The Captain kept on beating him. Then at last the horse stood motionless and gave a broken sigh. A pool of sweat darkened the pine straw beneath him and his head hung down. The Captain threw the whip away.

This fablelike confrontation is similar to a dream in its displacement of objects and roles, of latent and manifest content. The unexpected appearance of the soldier, stark naked, who looks at him with "vague impersonal eyes as though looking at some insect he had never seen before," reawakens both his hatred and his infatuation.

The scenes involving the Captain, the nude soldier and the horse have a dreamlike quality of portent, the meaning obscure but foreboding. We are prepared for a crime, but uncertain as to who will commit it. Thinking he has found the

Major in the bedroom of his wife, the Captain shoots the soldier, who is crouched beside the bed.

> . . . Even in death the body of the soldier still had the look of warm, animal comfort. His grave face was unchanged, and his sun-browned hands lay palms upward on the carpet as though in sleep.

This closing sentence might be seamlessly inserted into Stephen Crane's *The Red Badge of Courage*. A camera eye appears to scan the scene, and give us this detached, impersonal impression. Both writers knew the exact effect they wanted, and found the voice and the distance to realize it. Both tales are remarkable tours de force, technically audacious, relying on imagination to provide the substance and arouse the appropriate emotions. To *chime* these notes of emotion, to see life as it is, the actuality stern, mournful and fine, is more gratifying to the soul than argument or special pleading. When this is done successfully, the reader is left with the impression that he has seen more than what has been described, that he has, indeed, briefly glimpsed reality behind the veil of appearances. These images made of words, these artful impressions, appear to reduce life to the essentials, but their effect on the imagination is to enhance the essentials to a poetic truth.

> There was the sound of footsteps, and Honey Camden Brown stood on the threshold between the kitchen and the parlor. He wore tonight a yellow shirt with a bow tie, for he was usually a natty dresser—but his dark eyes were sad, and his long face still as a stone. F. Jasmine knew what Big Mama had said about Honey Brown. She said he was a boy God had not finished. The Creator had withdrawn His hand from him too soon. God had not finished him, and so he had to go around doing one thing and then another to finish himself up.

We do not see the hard facts of life in this light until they are transfigured by the image-maker. The world itself is unfinished until he goes around and finishes things up.

# Origins: The Self-Imaged Image-Maker

The telling imagery of our memorable writers is rooted in memory and emotion. The whiteness of the whale, the lineaments of death, the speech of groping hands, water purling over rocks, the recurrent voices of impotence and rage provide us with the clues to the writers' obsessions, the chimed notes of their emotion. In this wise, reader and writer are joined in a profound yet impersonal comprehension.

Before imagination supplements memory, it derives its energy from emotion, which is either positive and life-enhancing or negative and life-negating—in praise of life, or registering the first of many complaints. As the writer accumulates experience, craft and observation will enlarge memory, but the first impressions to emerge in his consciousness will often prove to be the last. They grow out of the compost of his nature, and prove to be a new species.

Much of my own plains-based fiction grew out of my need for an experience I came too late for. The town of Lone Tree itself, observed, in passing, in *The World in the Attic*, rose out of the need of a dwelling place for the likes of Tom Scanlon. Once that fact was apparent, the appropriate details assembled about his person—a hotel, a lone tree, a railroad and a cattle loader, objects that were destined to serve as icons. These artifacts constituted the "scene" in the way movable props served to "locate" a Western movie.

Like Uncle Fremont, in *Cause for Wonder*, I came too late for God and too early for the Farm Security Administration. A boy of nine, I left the Platte Valley ignorant of the fact that my hometown of Central City had once been called Lone Tree. This name had been abandoned as planted trees grew, and the town was well shaded for my boyhood. The fictive town of Lone Tree is an assemblage of parts testifying to my own homesteading program. Some of this fabrication is rooted in fiction, much of it my own, but all of it had been processed by the memories and emotions of my boyhood. The emotion would make of the shards of memory all that it could.

When we say "How well I remember!" invariably we remember poorly. It is the emotion that is strong, not the details. The elusive details are incidental, since the emotion is what matters. In this deficiency of memory do we have the origins of the imagination? To repossess we must imagine: our first memories are as dim as they are lasting. Until recorded history, memory constituted history and memory processed by emotion was our only means of repossession. When this is done with talent, we define it as art.

The faculty of memory, and the quality of emotion, varies from person to person and from writer to writer, making certain that what is remembered is a continuously expanding spectrum. The mind is often at play, like the summer night buzzing with insects, but to imagine, to make an image, to shape, assemble and structure experience, differs from the play of fancy and invention through the energy it receives from emotion. The image-making characteristic of science and fantasy fiction is largely free of this charge of feeling. The most remarkable events, inconceivable disasters, unheard-of creatures and identified flying objects pass through the mind without distressing the emotions. If the charge of feeling is present, it is no longer merely science-fantasy fiction. Those novels that once went along with hammocks, perhaps still described as "light summer reading," were crafty in the way the imagery was free of memory processed by emotion.

Image-making begins in earnest where memory fades. The skein of memory is often so frail we see right through it, and it frays at the edges. Invoking memory's presence may prove similar to a séance. Is it really *him,* we wonder, or an impostor? Imagination can be lured, but not willed, to do this restoration for us. In good fiction we can usually distinguish those portions that are craftily constructed from those winged with imagination. Without the gossamer of memory it is less than life; with it as a ground it proves to be more. First we make these images to see clearly: then we see clearly only what we have made. In my own case, over forty years of writing what I have observed and imagined has replaced and over-lapped what I once remembered. The fictions have become the facts of my life.

One of our necessary illusions is that we see things as a "whole." If we look at a map we see a confusion of criss-crossing lines, boundaries, and colors, in which the large details often prove to be the least noticeable. What country is it? This may prove difficult to determine. We must learn to read the map, as we do a face. We get a general impression, lacking details, or we get the details without the larger impression. A trained eye, of course, hopes to get both, as when the critic observes a painting, or the artist studies a landscape. What we see on the mind's eye of memory is seldom clearly one or the other. An overlapping of many impressions, as in a Cubist painting, creates a vibrant but jumbled image. The mind is an archive of these sensations. In their infinite variety they still exhibit individual and general characteristics. Nabokov says, "Speak, Memory!" But memory is not Hamlet's ghost. It is Nabokov who speaks. On this gauzelike memory tissue, and from those competing fragments, the writer chooses and reassembles his own pictures. The reader exclaims, "What a memory you have!" But it is what escaped memory that stirred the writer to write.

In the clutter of what is remembered and what is imagined

some things prove to be symbolic objects. They gather lint. They wear in rather than out.

A bent skate key
A needle with a burned point
A ball of tinfoil
A streetcar token (found among coins in a city without streetcars)
The cracked chimney of a lamp
A medal won for not smoking

Artifacts mystically quickened with sentiment await their reappearance in the imagination, a re-enactment and a confirmation. Each time these tokens are handled they give off sparks.

> . . . . On the dresser in the bedroom, where it ticked loudly, he would put out his railroad watch, on its chain, with the small gold knife that he used to clean the grease from his nails. Until he shaved at the kitchen window where just his lathered head showed above the curtain, he wore his snug whipcord pants with the straps of his braces dangling, his underwear unbuttoned to expose the crinkly hair on his chest. Nothing could have been more commonplace, but it left on Cowie a lasting impression. No ordinary mortal arose so late in the day and walked around as he did, wearing harness, as if unhitched from the work he had accomplished while asleep.

I was reluctant to surrender myself to this scene, feeling that I was spying on my own imagination. Unmentioned, but sharp to my senses, are the surrounding presence of a summer morning and the scorched smell of the iron on the draft from the kitchen. These memory fragments of separate, dispersed impressions have been filtered through a cherished emotion. At the window the swing creaks, the blind sucks in against the screen; water drips in the pan under the icebox.

The American writer, for self-evident reasons, often beginning with the disorder of creation, is "subject to the superstition that objects and places, coherently grouped, disposed for human use and addressed to it, must have a sense of their own, a mystic meaning to give out."

This testimony links Henry James to the object-and-place-obsessed imaginations of Whitman and Twain. Image-making exorcises this obsession. The crackle of singed hair, stretched across a lamp chimney, around which memories and emotions cluster, waits on the moment that imagination will release it from darkness. How appropriate it is that the fledgling writer tests his faculties on these first impressions. Soon enough he will see more than he remembers, and observe more than he imagines, but the clue to his image-making will be found among the objects with a mystic meaning to give out.

> When he was a kid he saw the town through a crack in the grain elevator, an island of trees in a quiet sea of corn. That had been the day the end of the world was at hand. Miss Baumgartner let them out of school so they could go and watch it end, or hide and peek at it from somewhere. . . . They stretched on their bellies and looked through a crack at the town. They could see all the way to Chapman and a train smoking somewhere. They could see the Platte beyond the tall corn and the bridge where Peewee had dived in the sand, and they could see T. B. Horde driving his county fair mare. They could see it all and the end of the world was at hand.
>
> The end of the world! he said.
>
> HOO-RAY! said Dean Cole.

Memory's chief contribution to this scene was the mood of apprehension and exhilaration, shared with a companion. School was dismissed, a priceless boon well worth the world's loss. Miss Baumgartner was a borrowed detail, as so many were, from my school days in Omaha, where I was older and more observant. I did not go up a ladder, as reported, since I feared all heights more than humiliation. Peewee and the bridge were a cherished rumor at the time of writing, but the scene grew out of a boy's elation at the prospect of a mind-boggling disaster. In this brief fiction I gained a shameful triumph over lost time.

Somewhat earlier in time:

> . . . That stovepipe came up through the floor from the coke burner in the room below, and where it bulged like a goiter it

would get hot when the damper was down. He could hear the coke crackle and settle when he turned it up. . . . All he wanted to do by turning the damper was to bring up the woman who lived below, the way the genie in the picture would rise out of Aladdin's lamp. She would come up with her lamp, the wick swimming in oil, and cross the room like the figures in his dreams, without noises, without so much as taking steps. Holding the lamp to his face she would see that he was asleep. He would feel the heat of the chimney on his forehead, catch a whiff of the oil. She would first open the damper, then turn with the lamp so that the room darkened behind her, but her snow white hair seemed to trap the light. During the day it would be piled on her head, but when she came up with the lamp it would be in braids. With a silver-handled comb that rattled when she used it, facing the mirror that no longer had a handle, she would comb out the tangled ends of her braids. Out would come, like the burrs in a dog's tail, the knotted hairs. When all the hairs stood up, like a brush, she would pass the ends slowly over the chimney, where they would curl at the tips and crackle with a frying sound. Then the smell, as when she singed a chicken over a hole in the range, or turned the bird, slowly, in the flame of a cob dipped in kerosene.

It is difficult for me, so long after the event, to penetrate the fiction to the original memory. I lie in bed under a sloping ceiling that seems to smoke and waver with looming, hovering shadows cast by a lamp. Out of my sight a woman hums snatches of hymns as she brushes her hair. The crackle I hear is made by the brush. On another occasion I watched her test the height of the flame in the lamp chimney by stretching one of her white hairs across the opening at the top. I still fancy I see its burning glow, like the filament of a light bulb. This simple scene has the primal elements that stir both the emotions and the imagination. There is light and darkness: there is mystery, wonder and a nameless apprehension. In her voice there is a comforting assurance. The moment is a ceremony. My child's soul is hushed with awe and a tremor of dread as I anticipate her mumbled, sonorous prayers. If I attempt to recall this actual occasion, the image blows like smoke, yet something hovers and protects me as if I were cradled at the mouth of a cave. The details are indistinct, but the emotion is inexhaustible.

To what extent is this true of later events, when the observed details are clearer? In the mid-fifties I visited Mexico, and spent a memorable week in Matamoros. Some years later this experience was the basis of a crucial chapter in *One Day*, published in 1965. A caged bird is intrinsic to this experience.

> A species of canary, Cowie's first impression had been that it was an object, made of cork and pipe cleaners. Artful, perhaps. No question it was horrible. There were quills, but no feathers, below the neck. The head with its lidded eyes was elevated on the neck like a lampshade. The legs and claws were twisted bits of wire. Cowie took it as an example of the Mexican taste for the macabre: the skull-and-bone cookies eaten by children, the fantastic birds and animals made out of paper. When he glanced up to see it headless, he simply thought the head had dropped off. But no. Nothing lay in the bottom of the cage. The head, with its knife-like beak, had been tucked under the quills of one wing. Fly it could not, lacking the feathers. Sing it would not. But on occasion it hopped.

Mexico is inexhaustibly exotic (for Americans), at once intoxicating and harrowing. The sensible and the absurd overlap, the grotesque is commonplace. For the writer this garden of macabre delights is both an inspiration and a disaster. In admitting to the surreal quality of his impressions, the writer must maintain the stance of a sober observer. Malcolm Lowry achieved this in *Under the Volcano*. My own hallucinated experience in Matamoros featured a large cage without a bird. Gazing at it and through it, over many days and nights, it became for me a symbolic object. Almost a decade later, repossessing it in fiction, Cowie's experience called for a bird. I imported one I had observed on a previous stay in Querétaro. The perfect setting for both the bird and the cage were provided by Matamoros. Cowie's Mexican adventure provided the author with the overview of many previous visits, as well as arresting and insoluble reflections that arise from the dismaying overlapping of extremes that are both life-enhancing and appalling. Without Matamoros none of this would have happened, but little of it actually occurred in Matamoros. The perfect cage had been found for the imagined bird.

In a recent novel, *A Life,* an old man returns to the New Mexico homestead where he had once raised sheep. As a young man, 1929, I had visited such a spot. My Texas uncle had wanted me to see the shack where he had brought his bride and made his start in life—as an example to a citified youth about to go to college in California. The site had impressed me as bleak, godforsaken and romantic, full of promise if the bride had been well chosen. In the deep ravine at my back the sky was reflected in the Pecos River. On the low rise before me, the color of rusted machinery, a two-room shack sat in a clearing. There they had lived. Everything else, he took pains to assure me, had died.

My actual memory of that visit is like a bad colored slide held to the light. Above a low dark horizon, without details, a brilliant metallic sky. At my back the purl of shallow water over rocks. That landscape of emptiness, joined to my inscape of emotion, furnished the scene with the artifacts that were lacking, appropriate to the old man's homecoming.

> The path he followed dipped sharply toward the river, then rose to the rim of the bluff where he had once bailed for water when his well dried up. At that point, as if a machine had collapsed, he found an assortment of iron wheels, one of the largest mounted on an axle across two wooden horses, a gulley trenched in the earth beneath it so the wheel would turn freely. To the outside rim of the wheel cans of various sizes had been bolted or wired. What did the builders have in mind? . . . Had they planned to irrigate? . . . He walked on to where a blowout had widened the trail at the top of the rise, a fine powdering of sand blowing into his face as he approached. Through half-lidded eyes, his gaze partially averted, he peered over the hump into the hollow where the sheep and their ewes often gathered to get out of the wind. It was now grassless, like a play yard, and strewn with the bodies and parts of wrecked cars. The colors of black and rust,

in the morning light, made him think of prehistoric monsters, this hollow a place where they came to die. Beyond, just above his eye level, the slope below the house had been terraced in the manner of rice fields. Where water had settled and evaporated it gleamed like exposed rock. A few shrivelled plants were supported by sticks; others had collapsed to lie in the dust. The house was there, or more accurately the cabin, to which lean-to shelters had been added, open to the yard. These stalls faced the southwest, were roofed with boards and tin, and sheltered parts of car bodies that served as furniture. The door of a sedan provided one room with an up and down cranked window; he could see that it was down. Torn strips of material that once might have served as awnings stirred in the breeze that always followed the sun's rise. The bands of color looked festive, like banners at roadside stands. Where was everybody? Was it so early they had not got up? He peered around for a dog before moving closer. The wind brought him the tinkle of glass chimes. Light glinted on the strips of glass and tin suspended on wires in the open doorway. A cart made of buggy parts, using the tree and the axles, featured old tire casings wired to the rims. Lengths of rope, attached to the front axle, were tied to a yoke that could be pulled by men, rather than horses. Directly fronting the house, where the terraces began, large cylindrical objects, like metal jars, were suspended on wires between heavy posts. The jars were graded in size, and put Warner in mind of the pipes of an organ, or something to be hammered. There was every sign of life but life itself, which he felt must be just out of sight somewhere, as if out of mind. At the top of two long tilted poles, reaching into the sun's rays, several gourds were hung from a crossbar, one of them slowly revolving. As it turned to the sun he saw a small bird enter one of the egg-sized holes.

The fragmented ruins of a hippie commune, where more than sixty years ago his own life had started, provide a suitably ironic setting for Warner's last impressions. All of these details are fictive, conjured up by the mingling of memory, imagination and emotion, ingredients that waited, like the old man, for their appropriate transformation.

The proliferating image of our time is the photograph. It is rapidly replacing the "abstraction" as the mirror in which we seek our multiple selves. Paradoxically, it was the photograph that inspired the emergence and triumph of the abstraction, freeing the imagination of the artist from his obsession with appearances. A surfeit of abstractions, and abstracted sensations, although a tonic and revelation for most of this century, has resulted in a weariness of artifice that the photograph seems designed to remedy. What else so instantly confirms that the world exists? We need this daily reassurance. Objects and places, whether coherently grouped or not, constitute the ambience in which we have our being. The photograph reaffirms, the cinema enshrines "the ineluctable modality of the visible." That also includes its abuses, the violence that functions as pornography of sensation. The film has also obscured, momentarily, that its representations, its imitations of life, are an old rather than a new form of image-making, and that the viewer is back to the startled point of his departure, the need for further image-making. In the dark cave of the theatre, like the child under a porch, he must re-imagine what it is he thinks he sees.

As we now know, language has its own purpose, and distorts in the act of being lucid. To a measurable degree, lucidity falsifies the truths of image-making. The emotion that fuels the imagination, and is in turn put to the service of individual experience, departs from the notion that the real world is there to be seized rather than reconstructed. The primal experience to which God might refer, as to a clear snapshot of the Garden of Eden, is precisely the image that is lacking. Adam and Eve have become image-makers out of necessity. The dreaming cat may have a clearer picture, to his own purpose, than the dreamer in whose lap he is curled, but he lacks the faculty of reassembly that distinguishes and terrifies the species homo. Nothing is, but image-making makes it so.

We see and document the microcosm of the atom, and we see and document the macrocosm of space. The likeness of one to the other is striking. It is not hard to imagine a point in space-time where these extremes met and joined. Fabulous, but not unimaginable. Not too long ago, if we can believe what we see, we saw planet Earth rising on the moon's horizon. Real as it appears, this image resists our abilities to grasp it. We might describe it as an object fallen from the sky, for which we lack the appropriate emotions.

Before we made fire, before we made tools, we made images. Nor can we imagine a time in which man has not had imagination. In the deep recesses of caves at Lascaux, Altamira, Pech Merle and elsewhere, prehistoric man proved to be an image-maker of baffling sophistication. The ceilings of these caves feature puzzling signs, as well as inspired representations of animals of the hunt. Horses and bison, the woolly mammoth, the reindeer are *imaged* in a manner we think of as modern. The audacity of the conception is matched by the refinement of the execution. Over a gap of twenty thousand years of silence they capture, as we say, our imaginations. We might guess that the artist's talent increased his self-awareness, his sense of uniqueness, distinguishing him from his companions, this in turn burdening his soul with an enlargement of his sense of wonder. The caves of Lascaux, as well as those in the bluffs along the river near Hannibal, Missouri, provided refuge for dreamers and image-makers inscrutably motivated to be more fully conscious. The caveman, the lunatic, the lover, the poet and the child under the porch, if he can find one, have at their instant disposal the inexhaustible powers of light and darkness, the ceaseless, commonplace, bewildering interlacing of memory, emotion and imagination. That's where it all comes from, and of the making of such fictions there will not soon be an end.

# Unearthly Adornments

The word "dream," for most Americans, does not describe hallucinations occurring during sleep, but a normal, euphoric state of waking. Daydreaming may well inhibit our interest in night dreaming. We find wakeful fantasies (I can dream, can't I!) more gratifying than inscrutable hallucinations. Night after night in deep slumber, or bobbing on sleep's undulant surface, the stage of the mind is the scene of a ceaseless and mystifying drama. The performance has neither a beginning nor an ending. It is at once a masque ball, a charade, a burlesque, an extravaganza, a miracle play. Unmistakably it is also always a dream. In spite of varying claims, of ceaseless interpretations, the scenario defies explanation. They are our first and will prove to be our last fictions. Predictably, the tormented and obsessed mind will deploy its energy in dream production, but the non-tormented and playful mind also dreams to sleep, and sleeps to dream. Here is the original and never-ending theatre of the absurd. In the imagination of a few men of genius we find a world of comparable splendor, but of limited resources. Dreams have access, as nothing else, to the inexhaustible. The study of dreams, understandably, has diverted both dreamers and observers from the heart of the matter. It is the *nature* of dreaming, the imagery of dreaming, not its burden of meaning that concerns the artist. Each dreamer is the sorcerer's apprentice in this production of images, a dazzled and compliant witness of the random and the involuntary.

Conceivably, if asked about his dreams, Hieronymus Bosch might have replied, "What dreams?" In the mind of his age, more visual than verbal, the lunatic, the lover and the painter were of one imagination compact. Bosch is merely one of many to have singular visions of earthly delights and torments. In the workshop of his imagination there were no separate compartments of suitable materials. Images were made out of everything at hand. With the increase of self-awareness, of analysis, the wakeful and the dreaming mind were seen in opposition. Shakespeare is at this watershed in the winds that blow in *The Tempest*. But this comes almost a century after "The Garden of Earthly Delights."

The medieval imagination, as revealed in Bosch, combined technical advances of the greatest refinement without a loss of "such stuff as dreams are made on." He is at once sophisticated and naïve, the happiest of circumstances for the obsessed image-maker. Was he able to marvel, as we are, at what he hath wrought? Or was it all in a long day's painting, a fabulous interweaving of the real and the imaginary? Nowhere else is the "real" world so prophetically foreshadowed in the dream world. In the lower right-hand corner of the triptych, a partially concealed crouched figure defecates coins into a cistern where other sinners are submerged. It is a minor detail, one of the numberless many easily overlooked.

We are dreamers, but few of us are good retrievers. Retrieving, unfortunately, is a talent in which the conscious image-maker plays a part. The retriever usually finds what he presumed to be lost. The dreams told to analysts, requiring interpretation, constitute a separate world of fiction. These recitals invariably lack what might prove to be of interest to the outsider. A parallel exists in the moviegoer who compulsively, and in detail, reports on all that he has seen. Part of the problem is technical: the verbal report is not visually commanding. We hear it, but we don't see it. At its point of origin this loss of detail may have given impetus to the arts of fiction. Everybody dreamed, but only the storyteller was able to hold the listener's attention.

As a writer of fiction and a wakeful-type dreamer, I am reluctant to give myself over to dreaming. It has made me a notably poor dream retriever. At best I salvage a few receding impressions, like those of a swimmer about to go under. I have been able to note, however, that these partially salvaged images resemble, in their intensity and vagueness, the images of conscious memory. Not in the bizarreness we recognize as dreaming, but in the way I sense that they come from the same workshop. In sleep, another hand deals the cards, but they are from the same deck.

Memory and dreams, in their conflicting needs, have access to the same archive of stored impressions. In the dream this confusion calls to mind an amateur theatrical production, featuring Goodwill costumes and remnant-sale handouts. It is still a moot point as to whether the dreamer has, or might have, access to inherited impressions, along with those personally acquired. It seems plausible, in such a mind as Bosch's, but it has not proved demonstrable. Much in our natures is genetically coded, but not in the context of images. We need not question, however, that dream fabrication contributes to conscious image-making, and that in the medieval imagination this contribution was overwhelming. Recently, the Surrealist painters have exploited these resources, but in the modern writer, with few exceptions, the dream is not a dream but a device that no longer serves its purpose. When the character says "I had this dream—" the reader is best advised to skip it. Actual dreams do not lend themselves to fiction, but the faculty of dream image-making is sorely absent from modern writing. Obsessed with what is *real*, with what he thinks to be real, the writer has little sympathy for what remains to be imaged. He is skeptical of the imagination, idolatrous of the facts. Until recently the writer has not been disturbed by the way the "real" recedes as he is about to grasp it, but an awareness is slowly emerging that the real world is a fiction awaiting the appropriate demonstration. In dreams begin the images of responsibility.

Those we call savages dance the wakeful dreams that Bosch paints with such remarkable detachment. The discipline and abandon of his imagination have encouraged study but discouraged imitators. One of his children might have asked him, "What is the world like, Papa?" and looked to his paintings for an answer. A few years after his death the question was asked:

What is the meaning, Hieronymus Bosch, of that frightened eye of
    yours?

The reasonable man, in both Bosch's time and ours, searches the painting for the dream scenario. There are numerous conflicting theories and speculations. In a century open to symbol hunters, there is no preserve for hunting the equal to this one. The problem is to fit Bosch into the world, rather than the world into Bosch. Four centuries after this dream of earthly life was portrayed as realistically as a peasant wedding, the study of dreams became an analytic and aesthetic obsession. Freud's description of money as human excrement is still too strong for sensible people, but the lunatic and the poet, if they were dreamers, might have guessed it.

The example of Bosch is so overwhelming that the lesson of the master has been counterproductive. Much of Surrealism might be tucked into one panel of his triptych. My interest is not in the enigma, the elusive meaning of his painting, or the use he made, if any, of astrology and witchcraft, or the liberties he took with traditional symbols, but in the faculty he exhibits to use all of these resources in his image-making.

The fantastic is often achieved, as a child might, by a simple inversion of scale: a cherry proves to be large enough to sit on, or carried about like a lantern. A single strawberry proves to be as large as a tree, a blackberry the size of a bush. Some birds are enormous, realistically painted; others fly and flock in their customary manner. Fish are everywhere; a few swim in the sky and others are carried about like trophies. This mingling of the commonplace and the bizarre, in both natural forms and hybrid creations, is the source of Bosch's enchantment. We feel it might all be an act of nature, observed by, but not invented by, the painter. So Adam and Eve might have felt if they had witnessed the first day of creation. God's intent, if not his argument, is not as yet codified and formulated. It is still a world of pure sensation. The grotesque forms impress us as organic, a form of life as real, or more real, than we are. They hold free sway over our imaginations because they are based on forms of nature. In his imitators the hybrid forms are too often merely fanciful, fantastic but lifeless, mechanical as the inventions of science fiction.

The magical ingredient in Bosch's creation is that it flows from an undivided imagination. There is not a real and familiar world by day, and an unreal suppressed world by night, but a universe in which these conflicting realities mingle, as they did in the minds of his contemporaries. We know that medieval life had its tableaux of horror, and that monsters were real as well as imaginary. In nearby Antwerp, Breughel would soon be painting a world as universal as that of Bosch, but even more disorderly and threatening, his painterly eye focused on the actual. Bosch's vision, like that which we find in the Bayeux tapestry, is meant to enchant as it instructs. Of the Italian painters of the fifteenth century Carpaccio might have marveled the most at his genius. He, too, combined the visionary with the earthly in a manner that effaced distinctions.

There is no precedent for the landscape in which "The Garden of Earthly Delights" is established. The horizon resembles the world he saw about him, the familiar and congenial face of nature. The visible horizon is broken, however, by two fantastic structures, one coral pink in color, the other of a steel blue, metallic in appearance. The hybrid mixture of forms, funguslike and organic, blends with the purely bizarre and imaginary. A profusion of marinelike ornaments, seed pods and spiky growths, gives one a festive air: it might be an ornament carried in celebrations, or waved by a child. Three similar but even more bizarre growths, larger because they are nearer, are set in or adjacent to the body of water that extends across the width of the panel. We are able to see that these structures serve as dwellings, and to guess that they also function as machines in the control or the flow of water. They are alike in combining forms that appear to be organic, crowned with flowers and curling tendrils that are leaflike, with details that suggest man-made constructions, yet having no parallel elsewhere. One is pierced near the base by hollow glass tubes, suggestive of receptacles or retorts for laboratory experiments; another, capped by a tower of marble and crystal shafts, appears to float. The most remarkable, gun metal in color, resembles a land mine or some machine of war, with screws that protrude like the barrels of guns. In the shadows at its base a tribe of monkeys seek for food. Topping this structure, like an enormous sundae, or the flower and fruit forms to ornament a hat, is a composition at once enchanting and demented. The luxuriance of fancy seems perverse. As his dazzlement cools, the observer asks, Is this a true creation or some trick of sorcery? Why these bizarre, fantastic eruptions? Has Bosch, in this way, succeeded in asking a larger, more disturbing question? Putting man aside, is it nature herself that has gone berserk? What we sense in these forms is a bacchanal in which nature is the victim, a ballet of forces and perversions in which the ailments of humankind are prefigured. These fantastic creations dominate the central panel and provide the clues to the drama unfolding in the middle and the foreground, God's world in a state of disorder having fallen from grace. The spirit of these forms is that of delight and abandon, but what is made visible is remarkably chaste. The swarming throng of nude humanity seems innocently appropriate to the landscape. Although a painter of realism comparable to Breughel, the conventions of a painterly morality limit Bosch to the use of symbols where he means to be explicit. The profusion of cherries, berries and strawberries symbolizes erotic and sensual delights. A courtly lady of refinement might have pondered this tableau with some misgiving but with a minimum of shock. The dream books of the time are detailed and explicit as to the meaning of berries and grapes, as well as the birds and sea fish signifying lewdness, lust and anxiety.

Has anyone since Bosch been so implicitly suggestive, and so explicitly chaste? The symbols of his Garden, like everything else, are subject to metamorphosis and mutation. This matchless portrayal of sexual suppression is equally in praise of sensual pleasure, nor is there any hint that the mind of Bosch took prudish delight in his swarm of sinners. Before they have fouled themselves, through weakness of the flesh, he seems to take delight in their prospects. It is a vision of man more charitable than the one that prevailed in his century: there is more of Erasmus and *humanitas* in it than the revenge of God. These are *earthly* delights, and his depiction of hell, in the third panel, is more prophetic of the facts of the twentieth century than a Dantesque horror chamber. Everything has gone from bad to worse, but we are still on earth. Fire and destruction loom in the background, where anonymous masses swarm about in disorder, a spectacle so common to modern man it is more familiar than horrifying. At the lip of this inferno, where the temperature is cooler, we pick up with what is left of the Garden of Earthly Delights. Beams of cold light flash on the sky like beacons, providing a suitable pallor for the tongues of hellfire. But life still goes on, however chaotic. The central figure of the panel is a huge, egg-shaped monster with two treelike limbs, peeled of their bark. The rear end of the egg gapes open to reveal, like the mouth of a cave, those who have found shelter within it. Nude, dark-skinned creatures sit at a table, and a peasant woman, fully clothed, takes ale from a barrel as if she means to serve them. On the chipped rim of the shell, leaning on it like a bridge rail, a man pensively meditates, his head resting on his hand. Is it Bosch? No other figure has such a resigned, contemplative posture. The head of the monster, however, the same pallor as the eggshell, is twisted about to look back along his body. To our amazement it is not the head of a monster, but might well be one of the painter's neighbors. His glance is more reflective than agitated. What he sees does not appall him. Of the numberless faces in this Garden, this one has the rudiments of a likeness. The expression is detached but observant, and I would guess him to be the painter.

As a rule, we might agree that hell is better depicted than described. The painter is able to convey an instant impression, as well as one that can be studied and pondered at leisure. Ultimately, however, both are pictures. What is described must be *imaged*. The writer takes the greatest pains that we *see* what he tells us. "Let me show you," says the writer, and the reader replies, "I see!" As profoundly as the mind may be coded for language it is in the interest of image-making. Dante and Bosch were both image-makers, recording their special triumphs. If Bosch had been under the thralldom of "reality" his imagination would have been blocked. Fortunately, there was no one at his painterly elbow to ask, "But is it real?" In his concerted effort to know what is real, or what he thinks to be real, the modern writer knows less and less of interest. The unicorn was real enough for the medieval mind, as the Loch Ness monster seems to be for some moderns. Both observers seek the confirmation of an "image"—the one seen in tapestries or paintings, and the one seen, or presumed to be seen, in photographs. For both, what is "real" is a matter of imagination. It is the image that matters. Does it enchant us, move us or mysteriously stir us?

At the start of the film *2001, A Space Odyssey*, we see primates hovering at the mouth of a cave, resembling one cowering beast with many small blinking eyes. This very real and visual image is supplemented by the surging swell of Strauss's music, an immaterial embodiment of the sensation of dawning, of something transfigured. The moment of terror and enchantment is brief, but impresses us as real. The film has this many-faceted capability and makes the most of it. For most of this century, the writer of fiction has willingly cut back on the supplemental music. The wick of his imagination has been trimmed to the scale and fashion of a realistic image. What has been done is extraordinary, but it is no longer enough.

In American practice our obsession with the "real" has had a depressing effect on the imagination. In assuming we know what is real, and believing that is what we want, we have curtailed the role of the image-maker and measurably diminished "reality." If we ask how Bosch, a master of the bizarre, habitually blends the real and the imaginary, the commonplace and the unheard of, the clue is provided in the word "garden." All that we see has grown, or is still growing. The fertility of his fancy is organic. Hybrid forms sprout and multiply like sports of nature. We will never know from where, and in what manner, his talent was nourished with such visions, but the technical means to his ends is there to be contemplated. The modern novel, with its unqualified freedoms, is not so free as Bosch to be imaginative. If we compare it with "The Garden of Earthly Delights," where the incongruous harmonizes with the ordinary, the exhaustively detailed fiction is but one panel of the triptych. The delights are diminished. The earthly increased. The soaring imagination leashed and hooded, like a falcon. It makes for more and more of what we know, and what we have, less of what we crave.

Of necessity what we seek is elusive, an image more life-enhancing than the one we have exhausted, an enlargement of delight, a shrinkage of drabness, whether made up of Angels, grotesques, or the shards of the commonplace. A poet's way to put it is to speak of imaginary gardens with live toads in them, imagery that memorably links the present, through Marianne Moore, to the gardens of earthly delights.

# Index